COLLABORATION
for
CAREER &
TECHNICAL
EDUCATION

Teamwork Beyond the Core Content Areas in a PLC at Work®

Wendy Custable · Paul C. Farmer

Foreword by Robert Eaker

Solution Tree | Press

a division of
Solution Tree

555 North Morton Street
Bloomington, IN 47404
800.733.6786 (toll free) / 812.336.7700
FAX: 812.336.7790

email: info@SolutionTree.com
SolutionTree.com

Visit **go.SolutionTree.com/PLCbooks** to download the free reproducibles in this book.

Printed in the United States of America

Library of Congress Cataloging-in-Publication Data

Names: Custable, Wendy, 1975- author. | Farmer, Paul C., 1958- author.
Title: Collaboration for career and technical education : teamwork beyond
   the core content areas in a PLC at work / Wendy Custable, Paul C.
   Farmer.
Description: Bloomington, IN : Solution Tree Press, [2020] | Includes
   bibliographical references and index.
Identifiers: LCCN 2019049366 (print) | LCCN 2019049367 (ebook) | ISBN
   9781949539677 (paperback) | ISBN 9781949539684 (ebook)
Subjects: LCSH: Career education teachers--In-service training--United
   States | Career education teachers--Professional relationships--United
   States | Technical education teachers--In-service training--United
   States. | Technical education teachers--Professional
   relationships--United States. | Career education--United States. |
   Technical education--United States. | Teaching teams--United States. |
   Teacher participation in curriculum planning--United States. |
   Education--Methodology.
Classification: LCC LC1037.5 .C87 2020 (print) | LCC LC1037.5 (ebook) |
   DDC 373.2/8--dc23
LC record available at https://lccn.loc.gov/2019049366
LC ebook record available at https://lccn.loc.gov/2019049367

Solution Tree
Jeffrey C. Jones, CEO
Edmund M. Ackerman, President

Solution Tree Press
President and Publisher: Douglas M. Rife
Associate Publisher: Sarah Payne-Mills
Art Director: Rian Anderson
Managing Production Editor: Kendra Slayton
Production Editor: Laurel Hecker
Content Development Specialist: Amy Rubenstein
Copy Editor: Kate St. Ives
Proofreader: Elisabeth Abrams
Text and Cover Designer: Abigail Bowen
Editorial Assistants: Sarah Ludwig and Elijah Oates

DEDICATION

I dedicate this book to my family, especially my husband and two boys, who inspire me to take risks, embrace challenges, and love life. I also want to share my appreciation for the amazing applied arts teachers at Adlai E. Stevenson High School. I am in awe of their drive and dedication to ensuring the success of every career and technical education student. Their hard work, creativity, and collaborative culture prove they are what all CTE teams should aspire to become. They motivate me to always bring my best self each and every day.

—Wendy Custable

I dedicate this book to my family, for they are my inspiration, my lighthouse beacon, my reason for being, and instill me with a passion for continued learning and growth as a person and as a professional. I picture my grandchildren's faces as I work with educators throughout the country, and I ask those educators if what they are doing is good enough for their families. Then I ask myself, with those little faces of my grandchildren dancing in my mind, Is it good enough for them? If not, let's get ready for the challenge of change. I further dedicate this book to all the phenomenal educators who have helped me grow and challenged my thinking about what's best for students in our schools. I have been blessed with a network of incredible educators who have become lifelong friends and pushed me to grow while supporting me in my efforts. I am humbled by the network of my friends and family who have often believed in me more than I have believed in myself, and for that reason I also dedicate this book to them. This book is also dedicated last but not least to all my CTE family. It's time for CTE to grow in leaps and bounds—we got this, we are CTE!

—Paul C. Farmer

ACKNOWLEDGMENTS

Solution Tree Press would like to thank the following reviewers:

Brian L. Ferguson
Assistant Principal
Mount Si High School
Snoqualmie, Washington

Lana Powers
Department Chair for Business,
  FACs, Fine Arts, and Technology
Central High School
Evansville, Indiana

Visit **go.SolutionTree.com/PLCbooks** to download
the free reproducibles in this book.

TABLE OF CONTENTS

Reproducible pages are in italics.

ABOUT THE AUTHORS

Wendy Custable, EdD, is the director of applied arts at the award-winning Adlai E. Stevenson High School in Lincolnshire, Illinois. She has been in education for twenty-one years, beginning her career as a technology education teacher. In her current role at Stevenson, she leads career and technical education and driver education teams in professional learning, curriculum and instruction improvement, formative assessment, proficiency-based grading, and social-emotional learning. In addition to her teaching and leadership roles, Wendy has presented at state and national conferences, as well as coauthored the book *Proficiency-Based Grading in the Content Areas*. Wendy earned a bachelor's degree in industrial technology education from Illinois State University, a master's degree in educational leadership from Northeastern Illinois University, and a doctorate in educational leadership from Loyola University Chicago.

Paul C. Farmer has worked in public education for over thirty-five years. He started his education career teaching autobody in Montgomery County Public Schools, Maryland. He has held multiple leadership roles including department chair, teacher specialist in career and technology education, assistant principal, principal, and project director of instructional technology integration. He retired from public education in Fairfax County Public Schools in Virginia.

Paul was the principal of Joyce Kilmer Middle School, one of the first schools in the county to build and sustain the PLC at Work model. Kilmer was one of fifty schools in the United States recognized by Standard and Poor's School Evaluation Services for narrowing the achievement gap between economically disadvantaged students and the general population.

Paul now leads professional development focused on creating and sustaining Professional Learning Communities at Work and Response to Intervention at Work for teachers, school administrators, and district administrators throughout the United States and Canada. He coauthored *How to Help Your School Thrive Without Breaking the Bank* and *Dealing with the Tough Stuff: Practical Solutions for School Administrators*.

Paul earned his bachelor of arts in business management at National Louis University in Chicago, Illinois, and his master's in secondary education leadership at George Mason University in Fairfax, Virginia.

To book Wendy Custable or Paul C. Farmer for professional development, contact pd@SolutionTree.com.

FOREWORD

By Robert Eaker

As the popularity of both the Professional Learning Communities (PLC) at Work process and career and technical education (CTE) programs have grown in recent years, so have questions regarding how they each can enhance and support each other. It's not unusual for educators seeking to re-culture their schools into professional learning communities to ask, "How does the career and technical education program fit into the PLC at Work process?" The good news is that Wendy Custable and Paul C. Farmer provide a detailed answer to this and many other questions. *Collaboration for Career and Technical Education: Teamwork Beyond the Core Content Areas in a PLC at Work* provides educators with an in-depth analysis of how PLC at Work processes can enhance CTE programs, as well as how career and technical education can play an important role in implementing PLC concepts and practices throughout the school. Importantly, their work also provides specific strategies and examples for doing the work of embedding proven PLC practices into CTE programs.

One of the more challenging aspects of incorporating PLC practices into CTE programs is forming highly effective teams. Collaborative teams are the engine that drives a professional learning community, so the question is, If each of the CTE teachers only teaches one subject, how can they be organized into highly effective teams? The answer lies in the fact that there is no one right way to organize teams in a school's CTE program. Many schools have found ways of effectively teaming their CTE programs, and Custable and Farmer provide multiple examples of how readers can successfully address the teaming issue.

With teams effectively organized within a CTE program, the next question is, What do these teams do? The short answer is that CTE teams do what all high-functioning teams do within a professional learning community—they focus on the learning of each student, skill by skill. And, while CTE programs face unique challenges, CTE teams offer distinct advantages regarding the critical questions teams must address when ensuring high levels of student success (DuFour, DuFour, Eaker, Many, & Mattos, 2016): What is essential that all students learn? How will we know if they are learning it? How will we respond to those who are struggling with their learning? And, how will we respond to students who demonstrate proficiency? Custable and Farmer provide a detailed road map for doing the work related to each of these critical questions.

If teams truly want all of their students to learn at high levels, the first task is to clarify what all students must learn in each subject or course. In this regard, CTE teams have an advantage over what are generally referred to as the "core" academic subjects where state standards are often too broad, or too vague, or simply too many. Generally, the industry standards that are available in most CTE program areas are more useful because they go beyond simply stating a standard; they describe what student work should look like if a student is successful. Many core academic teams fail to take this step.

In addition to this increased clarity around essential learning and what success looks like, Custable and Farmer point out that successful teaching in CTE programs involves frequent formative assessment, feedback, and encouragement *during* the teaching process. Formative assessment is not a separate activity, but rather something that occurs naturally as part of the teaching and learning process. Formative assessments can be further enhanced when teams collaboratively develop them and analyze the results. The PLC at Work process enhances formative assessment practices within CTE programs by extending the purpose and effectiveness of collaboratively developed formative assessments. The act of collaboratively writing common assessments forces teams to sharpen their thinking about what students should learn. These assessments also enable teams to provide specific assistance to specific students regarding specific skills with which they are struggling. Equally important, the use of common formative assessments enables teams to analyze their own instructional effectiveness and set meaningful improvement goals—both short term and long term.

Issues such as these and many others are addressed in *Collaboration for Career and Technical Education: Teamwork Beyond the Core Content Areas in a PLC at Work*. James Collins and Jerry Porras (1997) observed that leaders often fall victim to the tyranny of *or*—choosing between two good ideas, concepts, or initiatives—rather than opting for the genius of *and*. Custable and Farmer's work demonstrates why PLCs *and* CTE can and should work together. Equally important, they show us how to successfully embed PLC practices into CTE programs. The only remaining issue facing educators is simply getting started and getting better!

INTRODUCTION

It is well known that the Professional Learning Community (PLC) at Work process increases levels of student learning, and the PLC movement continues to gain momentum and respect among researchers and educational organizations due to its positive impact on learning institutions. As Richard DuFour and Robert Marzano (2011) make clear: "The potential of the PLC process to improve schools has repeatedly been cited not only by researchers but also by professional organizations that serve as advocates for teachers and principals" (p. 21).

Though the PLC process includes all educators, much that has been written about the topic addresses or is most easily applied to core academic subjects and the teachers of those subjects. Although there continues to be a worldwide emphasis on academic learning and testing, most educators and parents will acknowledge there is more to educating students than academics alone. As teachers and leaders of career and technical education (CTE), we need to help other educators, employers, community members, students, and parents increase their awareness of the value of CTE. Many stakeholders recognize that CTE is important because it prepares students for college *and* careers. This is true, but it is not the only value to CTE. When students have a concentration of CTE on their transcripts, they have multiple avenues to pursue as they move into adulthood. Further, a CTE background provides skills and benefits that will last a lifetime. The following list shows lifelong skills learned in CTE programs of study. Some skills are unique to certain CTE pathways while others are more general to any CTE program of study.

- Apply for grants and scholarships.
- Secure and sustain an income.
- Network with people you don't know.
- Introduce yourself to potential employers.
- Present ideas and new concepts.
- Work as a member of a team.

- Manage general finances.

- Reconcile bank statements.

- Set up and monitor personal budgets.

- Apply for credit and loans.

- Be an entrepreneur.

- Use and maintain hand tools.

- Use and maintain power equipment.

- Read and understand technical information.

- Assemble and repair household items.

- Install household appliances.

- Demonstrate workplace etiquette.

The PLC process has been proven to strengthen learning in core academics, and CTE can also strengthen professional learning communities. Career and technical education teachers and teams consistently search for meaningful ways to become more effective, respected, and integrated into the vital systems and processes of PLCs.

PLCs and CTE have similarities in their growth in popularity and recognition in the 21st century. CTE is gaining momentum throughout many parts of the world; for example, Australia, Russia, countries in Western Europe, countries in Central Africa, and others have a significant focus on CTE, also known as vocational education (Association for Career and Technical Education, n.d.). In 2019, the United States Congress reauthorized the Carl D. Perkins Career and Technical Education Act of 2006 with a supporting budget of 1.2 billion dollars per year (Perkins Collaborative Resource Network, n.d.b). With this funding the government is asking every state to improve several aspects of CTE. There is an expectation to embed academics, prepare students for careers and college, and be nimble with responses to the local job market's needs by providing industry-ready and well-prepared employees. The following list mentions several but not all of the expectations for improvement in CTE (*Carl D. Perkins Career and Technical Education Act of 2006*, 2019).

- Develop more fully the academic knowledge and technical and employability skills of secondary education students.

- Develop challenging academic and technical standards and assist students in meeting such standards.

- Include preparation for high-skill, high-wage, or in-demand occupations in current emerging professions.

- Develop, implement, and improve career and technical education.
- Promote the development of services and activities that integrate rigorous and challenging academic and career and technical instruction.
- Conduct best practices that improve career and technical education programs of study, services, and activities.

CTE programs play an instrumental role in schools by offering a rich curriculum that connects students to core content, college, employment, and other real-life experiences. Embedding PLC processes in CTE programs of study can have an impact in meeting national and local community expectations of CTE. With the research supporting the PLC process for improving schools along with the support and demand for CTE to improve, partnering PLC and CTE efforts should improve both. DuFour and Marzano (2011) state, "The best strategy for improving schools and districts is developing the collective capacity of educators to function as members of a professional learning community" (p. 21). However, in our experience, we have witnessed the attempt by some schools to establish a PLC culture with a clear absence of CTE and other singleton teachers. In fact, in some cases, schools only use their CTE programs and teachers to house or supervise students while other teams collaborate. This needs to change or at least be reversed occasionally so teams with CTE representation can collaborate.

For example, we have observed in some schools a perception that the CTE courses are not as important as core academics. This perception is perpetuated when states do not have accurate methods to measure the effectiveness of CTE curricula and success as they do for academic subjects. However, in most of these cases the district or school decision makers have not been exposed to effective approaches of integrating CTE teams into PLC processes. This is a perfect opportunity for these leaders to start from scratch with the integration of CTE programs of study.

CTE teachers functioning in a PLC is not as easy as it may sound and will require a shift in the culture of the team to create collective commitments to the collaborative processes. In *Starting a Movement*, Kenneth C. Williams and Tom Hierck (2015) describe how to build a PLC and acknowledge that changing the culture to accept working together is not easy: "Working together is a lot more challenging than working alone. Focusing on what we as teachers can do instead of on what we don't have requires a collective commitment" (p. 1). However, teachers working interdependently within collaborative teams is not a fad. PLCs lead a movement in education that is changing how teachers work together for the success of their students. For a movement like this to pay off in schools, it must involve all teachers, including CTE teachers.

This book will explicitly describe how PLC processes that are often coveted for academic courses can be applied in a CTE context. Throughout the following chapters, we integrate PLC processes into CTE programs of study, reinforcing the research base of PLC processes while honoring the intent of CTE programs to prepare students for college and career. In our effort to clearly communicate the integration of PLC processes with CTE we provide numerous CTE-specific resources and reproducible worksheets throughout this book. If you are well versed in PLC, you will recognize many of the processes as similar to those covered in other PLC-related publications.

Moving CTE Teams Past Their Differences

CTE collaborative teams are different from those in other content areas where there are two or more teachers teaching the same content. Moving CTE teams past their differences will require some special consideration focused on finding commonalities. Even in schools that do include CTE teachers within their PLC culture, there is often very little understanding of how to support the work of these unique teams. In *Transforming School Culture*, Anthony Muhammad (2009) writes that the PLC process involves securing or creating a culture of an unwavering belief by all stakeholders that all students can learn at high levels and clear and concise policies and procedures to achieve the belief. Philosophically, this makes sense for CTE teams—all teachers within an assigned team work interdependently toward shared goals to improve the learning of all the students they serve. Practically, though, this can be a high hurdle for CTE teams when the teachers might not have common curricula or students.

So, how do CTE teachers move past their differences to form purposeful, high-functioning collaborative teams? This book is designed to provide the clarity of purpose and procedures for collaboration that will help teachers who don't have content partners work within a team. For CTE teams to find their purpose together, they need to find their common denominators—the content, skills, and behaviors that bring their otherwise very different curricula together for a common purpose. These common denominators might be unique to your CTE team or school, but they do exist, and you can find them if you are willing to collaborate on what you have in common. This means the team members will need to discipline themselves to think past all the differences in order to discover what they do share. The common denominators of an eclectic team may or may not be standards or finite skills within the different curricula, but the CTE team can identify commonalities from one program of studies to the next. A team's common denominators may also be focused on class management, instructional processes, student or adult behaviors, or curricula that are expected across programs.

Working as a collaborative CTE team requires teachers to be highly committed to continually improving student learning, their own learning, and the learning of their teammates. This work might not be easy at first—but the payoff for student learning in technical education programs that set them up for college and career success is well worth the work.

Getting the Most Out of This Book

Although this book is intentionally focused on integrating PLC processes with CTE teams or teams with CTE representation, any reader interested in learning more about best practices within a PLC will find the information, protocols, and templates useful. A team might include several CTE teachers of the same or similar courses, or it might be one CTE teacher working with teachers of music, physical education, or other areas. Readers will find an abundance of strategies for singleton teachers (those who are the only ones who teach their subjects and are therefore on teams with teachers who don't teach the same things) and for teachers who share the same programs of study with others on their team. These strategies are also appropriate for school leaders to learn, especially administrators who supervise teams with CTE representation.

Each chapter explains strategies and processes for cyclical operations for CTE teachers in a PLC. The topics we present are closely interrelated, and many processes are prerequisites for later chapters. The PLC process in CTE will function well when all aspects are present and executed with fidelity. Even so, different teams may start their journeys in different places and add components along the way. The intent of this book is to help schools change their PLC approach to include CTE with PLC efforts in an ongoing manner, not a one-and-done activity.

Chapter 1 examines the three big ideas of PLC culture and the four critical questions of collaborative teams and how readers can integrate them into a CTE team's culture and routines. This includes methods to help CTE teams focus on the right work as they collaborate—the right work being how to increase student learning.

Chapter 2 provides clarity on how to bring teachers from different subject areas together into a high-performing collaborative team. The rest of the work in this book hinges on teachers functioning in true collaboration with other professionals. This chapter clarifies what collaboration is as well as what to do with collaborative time.

Chapter 3 examines the logistics of collaboration. When teacher teams have clarity regarding their existence as a team, they are ready to refine the logistics of their collaborative time. This chapter covers many aspects of collaborative work, such as record keeping, roles in team meetings, schedules, norms for collaborating, and commitments between meetings.

Chapter 4 focuses on the content and on how to find essential learning that is common to members of the CTE team who don't teach the same program of study. The essential learnings we discuss are program specific and can include soft skills students must learn. This chapter includes unwrapping the technical jargon in the curriculum to show how it will be learned in a classroom and understood by the students. It discusses learning targets along with methods to identify learning targets in the essential learner outcomes. This chapter will help teachers develop commonality in effective teaching strategies on common essential learnings from class to class.

Chapter 5 covers the development of assessments and how to use them to confirm students are learning the essential outcomes. This chapter provides examples of aligning assessment questions to learner outcomes and references to test blueprints to inform the team of what is necessary for success on a high-stakes assessment. It also covers different types of assessments, assessment cycles, instruction and assessment plans, and calibrating scoring processes.

Chapter 6 addresses reflecting on data, which is where many collaborative teams get tripped up. This chapter focuses on what to do with the data from assessments and how to set up SMART goals (strategic and specific, measurable, attainable, results oriented, and time bound). It also includes different ways to analyze assessment results and provides strategies to put the data to work, rather than working for the data.

Chapter 7 furthers the use of data to set up intervention and enrichment systems. In addition to clarifying a schoolwide pyramid of interventions, we also describe how to set up intervention models within the CTE team or the classroom.

Finally, appendix A presents a glossary of terms while appendix B provides numerous reproducible worksheets and tools that CTE teams can use to enact the concepts from this book. Each chapter concludes with a set of vital action steps for your team to utilize as they create their new norms.

We encourage you to make the most of this book in three ways.

1. Use the strategies at the conclusion of each chapter (in the sections titled Vital Action Steps for CTE Teams) to reflect on how you might improve your team.

2. Plan time within the school year to experiment with structuring team meetings with the proposed protocols. As you become more comfortable using these collaborative protocols to structure your team conversations, customize them to meet the unique needs of your team.

3. Use the reproducible tools to increase your team's organization and to hold yourself and your team accountable to establishing a collaborative team culture.

CHAPTER 1

Establishing a Collaborative Culture

Creating a culture that willingly accepts changes and challenges, makes no excuses, and continues to seek ways to improve student learning can be daunting. This chapter discusses clarification of common language used in a PLC. If schools can incorporate the use and application of PLC language into daily operations, leaders can instill the belief in staff that this work is possible and will make a difference. The work ethic of CTE teachers is not usually a problem. What can cause an unhealthy culture is when teachers feel they are putting in the maximum effort but not all students are succeeding. As an example, when 20 percent of the students are performing below proficiency and the teachers are confident they are giving 100 percent of their effort, it can become frustrating and lead to a defeatist attitude. This unhealthy culture can serve as a launching point to openly discuss the problems and examine technical changes. Shifting out of a maintain-status-quo culture will require technical changes, but a culture must be in place that believes in, accepts, and utilizes the technical changes to their fullest. As Muhammad (2009) explains, "Substantial cultural change must precede technical change" (p. 16). Some educators may argue to address the technical changes first; others say culture first. Changing culture is about changing values and beliefs, and the willingness to try new and different approaches, while technical changes concern processes, strategies, and structures. Regardless of your choice about what gets done first, both forms of change need to take place and dovetail with each other. If technical changes are to be successful, the culture of the team must be ready and willing to try the technical changes with an open mind.

Some teachers—and even administrators—have posed the following question to us many times: Why should CTE teachers be included in our school's PLC initiatives? Our quick response is either "Why not?" or "Because it just makes sense to embrace research-based best practices on routines and structures to achieve high levels of student learning." The structures and processes of PLCs improve learning for students and teachers, improve the culture of the school, and improve graduation rates, which we believe leads to greater job satisfaction for teachers and increased postsecondary education achievement for students. Seeing this happen year after year, it just makes sense that CTE should be included in a school's efforts. If the processes of teachers working collaboratively within teams are the right thing to do for student learning in the core areas, then they are the right thing to do for student learning in CTE. Furthermore, a secondary purpose for CTE teachers working within collaborative teams is that research supports the belief that working within a collaborative team is one of the best forms of professional learning for teachers because it "promotes achievement, positive interpersonal relationships, social support, and self-esteem" (Hattie, 2009, p. 213). Working within collaborative teams improves collegial relationships in ways that lead to teacher actions that improve student learning, which is exactly what CTE has always been: practical.

Defining Professional Learning Communities

We should first define *PLC*, before we further discuss what it can be in CTE and why CTE is, in fact, critical for a healthy PLC. Richard DuFour, Rebecca DuFour, Robert Eaker, Thomas Many, and Mike Mattos (2016) define PLC as "an ongoing process in which educators work collaboratively in recurring cycles of collective inquiry and action research to achieve better results for the students they serve" (p. 10). A PLC is not a thing—it is not a meeting, or a day of the week, or a subcommittee. It is a campuswide lifestyle with unique structures, processes, procedures, and an interminable commitment to high levels of learning for all students.

While the preceding definitions include all members of a school community in the PLC process, many teachers assume PLC is only for core academics. If you find your team believes PLC is only for academic subject areas, a slight modification of DuFour and colleagues' (2016) definition is more explicitly inclusive (our addition and emphasis):

> PLC is an ongoing process in which educators *from all grades and content areas* work collaboratively in recurring cycles of collective inquiry and action research to achieve better results for the students they serve.

This statement signals to noncore areas like CTE that PLC is important for them as well.

With this inclusive approach, no teacher, teacher team, content area, or anyone earning a paycheck on campus is exempt from the operations of the PLC. In our schools, anyone who earns a paycheck is automatically considered a member of our PLC. We cannot emphasize enough that a PLC is not a team, it's a lifestyle. This approach sets the expectation that PLC is not just about the core content areas or isolated to certain processes, structures, routines, programs, or grade levels. As such, a PLC should absolutely include CTE. Williams and Hierck (2015) explain that when the work of PLC "feels like one more thing to do then it is just that; a shift from doing a PLC (compliance) to becoming a PLC (commitment) is necessary" (p. 4). Including all staff is an essential aspect of that commitment and, contrary to what some might think or claim, it is not overly difficult to incorporate CTE into the PLC process.

In addition to including all educators, PLCs focus on high levels of learning for all students. When we say "high levels of learning for all students," we refer to grade-level learning and above that prepares all students for careers and postsecondary education. Some

> **In our schools, anyone who earns a paycheck is automatically considered a member of our PLC.**

teachers might argue that it is impossible to provide high levels of learning for all students, citing students with cognitive deficits or other learning needs. It might be unreasonable to expect students with significant cognitive impairments to learn grade-level content, so we take the approach that Austin Buffum, Mike Mattos, and Janet Malone (2018) take: "we should define *all* as any student who can or might be an independent adult someday" (p. 46). Students who may not grow to become independent adults still receive an equally focused education; their education will need to be modified and tailored to meet their unique needs, which may not be typical for the general student population. These students' teachers would equally benefit from working in collaborative teams to determine the best practices to meet their students' needs.

If they accept this definition of *all*, PLC schools must commit to preparing all students to earn a high school diploma and be accepted into a postsecondary school or into a career with growth potential and benefits. Some schools add acceptance to the military to the list of acceptable student outcomes. Schools must stop the pre-identification processes that attempt to determine a student's future once they leave high school. Instead, educators must prepare students for any avenue they choose to pursue after graduation from high school. Whether that avenue leads to a postsecondary degree or immediate participation in the workforce, students should have the skills that allow them options and to evolve identities for themselves and their futures as they learn.

Defining Career and Technical Education

Like most educational terminology, career and technical education (CTE) has undergone many changes in name and meaning. CTE programs of study have been called *industrial arts*, *vocational education*, *trade and industrial education*, and so on. With those different titles, the fundamental purposes have changed as well. We prefer the following definition from the Glossary of Education Reform (2014).

> Career and technical programs—depending on their size, configuration, location, and mission—provide a wide range of learning experiences spanning many different career tracks, fields, and industries, from skilled trades such as automotive technology, construction, plumbing, or electrical contracting to fields as diverse as agriculture, architecture, culinary arts, fashion design, filmmaking, forestry, engineering, healthcare, personal training, robotics, or veterinary medicine.

Most school systems offer career pathways which include multiple programs of study throughout a student's school experience, and many are mixed with academic course requirements for career pathways completion.

Misconceptions About CTE

Regrettably, there are still schools where CTE is considered a place to send students to increase their GPAs because the work is supposedly easy. Other schools see their CTE programs as a place to send students who are struggling in other courses. Buffum et al. (2018) state:

> We find that many schools currently remove students from college-prep coursework and place them into vocational tracks, because they deem the student incapable of succeeding on a college-prep track. Vocational pathways can be an outstanding pathway to postsecondary education, but students should leave high school with the academic skills and behaviors necessary to succeed in university and vocational settings. (p. 130)

Unfortunately, we must acknowledge that the separation between vocational and academic courses has widespread acceptance in some communities and among some educators. There are cases where even educators will say that CTE is for low-performing students who will grow up to become low-paid, blue-collar workers. As with anything else, once a person's perception has been cast, it is difficult to change.

If you happen to be associated with people who feel CTE programs of study are for lower functioning students or lead to lower income employment and you want to help them see things a bit differently, consider the occupational employment statistics from the U.S. Bureau of Labor Statistics (available at www.bls.gov/oes/oes_emp.htm). This is a great resource to see income potential by trade in different states and localities, as well as the level of demand for that workforce. Another way to demonstrate the value of CTE programs is to ask local employers if they feel they have a highly skilled labor force to draw from when they have a vacancy. In our experience, the answer is often *no* and this is a good indication of the need for excellent CTE programs. The bottom line is that high-quality grade-level or advanced CTE programs help prepare students for postsecondary two-and four-year degree programs and immediate gainful employment with benefits.

> **There is no reason for a CTE teacher or department to be exempt from the PLC process and no excuse for schools attempting to exclude CTE from the PLC process.**

The goal of the CTE team is to prepare students for life by ensuring high levels of learning—no different from the goals of any academic subject. Therefore, there is no reason for a CTE teacher or department to be exempt from the PLC process and no excuse for schools attempting to exclude CTE from the PLC process. To close this section, it's good to keep in mind what a PLC is: "an ongoing process in which educators work collaboratively in recurring cycles of collective inquiry and action research to achieve better results for the students they serve" (DuFour et al., 2016, p. 10). This certainly sounds like a natural fit for CTE.

The Importance of CTE in a PLC

The reasons CTE is critical for a healthy PLC are numerous. The following are just a few examples.

- Industrialized nations are under constant pressure to increase the rigor of academic, technical, employability, and college and career readiness skills to prepare students for high-demand, high-skill, high-wage employment. By its very nature, CTE can make great contributions to the efforts of a PLC on this front.

- CTE curricula embrace 21st century workplace skills and demonstrate connections between academic skills and workplace success; this benefits students in all their classes and thus strengthens any PLC.

- CTE can contribute an abundance of non-fiction curricula such as charts, graphs, manuals, recipes, advertisements, letters, and newspaper articles, just to name a few. Focusing on non-fiction materials has significant impact on increasing student learning (Goodwin & Miller, 2013).

- CTE offers real-life connections between success in school and success in employment. These experiences give students greater opportunities to make personal and professional connections because CTE curricula are associated with skills that will result in financial success and independence, which has potential to create authentic interest and increase motivation.

These contributions from CTE teachers and teams benefit the entire PLC because CTE focuses on college and career readiness. Not all students are going to go directly to the workforce after high school, just as not all students will go to college. It is not a matter of the core academic curriculum or CTE being better than the other. Rather, they should complement one another. Not everyone has the ability or interest to be a philosophy professor or an autobody technician, but when the two professions are seen as different but of equal value (rather than different and of unequal value), the learning community gains substance, dynamism, and good will that lead to creativity, growth, and the best possible outcomes for students.

Once the case has been made for involving CTE in PLC, it is time to work on developing a common language among all stakeholders, starting with the three big ideas of a PLC.

The Three Big Ideas of a PLC

A PLC operates under the umbrella of three big ideas (DuFour et al., 2016):

1. A focus on learning
2. A collaborative culture and collective responsibility
3. A focus on results

Before reading this section, write down your working definition of these three phrases. After reading this section, have a team meeting and ask each member who is working through this book to bring their own written definitions to the meeting.

Engage in a collaborative discussion with the goal of creating a shared definition for each phrase. A worksheet to guide this process appears in appendix B (page 150). Be sure each team member has a voice in sharing his or her definitions and in the development of the team definitions.

In combination, the three big ideas encompass the work that takes place in the day-to-day operations, regardless of the content area or even if curricular content is not the focus. Constant reference to these ideas will help focus the efforts of a team with CTE representation. The first big idea, a focus on learning, is just that: there will be an intense and relentless focus on learning by all, meaning students and staff alike. The second big idea, a collaborative culture and collective responsibility, is a professional practice to determine and commit to best practices to reach increased levels of student and adult learning. This includes not only instructional practices but also instructional environment practices. For our purposes, the instructional environment is where the learning takes place, and environment-focused discussions may include setting up routines in a classroom or lab, organizing students, structures conducive to student learning, seating arrangements, workflow, and so on. Working in a collaborative culture helps to build the team's capacity for taking collective responsibility to get the work done. The third big idea is a focus on results. Teams must track outcomes in order to measure their effectiveness. Using results is foundational to creating goals, monitoring progress, identifying and celebrating goal achievement, and developing plans for continuous improvement.

The following sections take a closer look at how the three big ideas apply to teams of CTE teachers or teams that include CTE teachers.

A Focus on Learning

When it comes to a focus on learning for CTE teachers, there are two primary considerations. First and foremost, one must gain absolute clarity about what students will learn as a result of the teaching that takes place in a CTE program. To be clear, this is a focus on what students will learn in a CTE program of study, rather than how the teacher will cover every topic in the curriculum. Unfortunately, a focus on student learning is the opposite of typical efforts; many teachers, or even supposed teams, tend to focus on teaching, and once the teaching is accomplished, they move on. In a PLC, teams focus on what students will learn, and when the expected learning doesn't take place, they build in systems of intervention to guarantee the essential learning does take place.

Some teachers may say they already know what students will learn in this course—it's called the curriculum. However, Marzano (2003) discusses research suggesting there are three types of curricula: intended, implemented, and attained. The differences are as follows.

- The *intended curriculum* is what's written in a curriculum guide by the state, district, or other sources.
- The *implemented curriculum* is what is taught in the instructional environment.
- The *attained curriculum* is what the students actually learn and retain.

Having taught CTE ourselves with an intended curriculum based on standards, we identified specific learning targets and clarified success criteria, but we both realized that, at best, all we could really do was cover the curriculum—and even that proved impossible. It can be frustrating for a teacher when he or she experiences the inability to attend equally to all the standards. However, research reinforces that there are too many standards to be taught and learned in the amount of time available (Marzano, 2003). Having acknowledged this research, teachers are forced to clarify which parts of the intended curriculum will become the implemented curriculum, and which are essential for students to attain. A focus on learning means to clarify and commit to these essential learning targets. Team members hold themselves and each other accountable to make sure the students attain the essential skills in the implemented curriculum. It is important to emphasize that this approach is very different from what occurs in most schools, where the focus is on what will be delivered or covered in a class. If we don't change our priorities in this area, we would need to say the first big idea is to deliver or cover the curriculum. That is not what a focus on learning is about.

These essential learning targets would be considered the teacher's or team's *guaranteed and viable curriculum* (Marzano, 2003). The guaranteed and viable curriculum is what all students in a CTE program of study will have access to, with adequate time to learn and multiple opportunities to demonstrate what they learned. For example, when using power equipment, certain procedures for proper and safe use are nonnegotiable. Teachers must ensure that students know how to safely use a band saw, for example. The procedures will be retaught as many times as necessary until the student can demonstrate a consistently safe use of the band saw. Very often before a student can use power equipment, he or she must pass a verbal and written assessment about safety. Then, the student's first use is under the direct supervision of the teacher to confirm the student knows how to safely use the saw.

A guaranteed and viable curriculum also provides students with clarity on where to increase their attention and provides teachers with clarity on what to emphasize during instruction. Students do not have to prioritize the information presented to them; instead, the teacher provides that clarity because the teacher is the qualified expert in that content and has worked with his or her team to define the guaranteed curriculum. Teachers communicate the essential content, and these learnings will be guaranteed for all students in attendance. This is different from *opportunity to learn*. In many schools, students have an opportunity to learn everything covered, but in a non-PLC school, students also have the opportunity *not* to learn.

The second consideration for a focus on learning is teachers—the learning the CTE team does. Learning together when a team is figuring out what to do and when (along with deciding what skills must be guaranteed for the students to learn) will take commitment and buy-in, both of which can only be acquired when the members learn together. DuFour and colleagues (2016) state, "A cardinal rule of decision making in a professional learning community is that prior to making a decision, people must first build shared knowledge, that is, they must learn together" (p. 28). A focus on learning in a PLC includes a focus on the adult learning.

When a team of teachers has absolute clarity on which specific knowledge or skills students will learn, the team can work collaboratively on the best strategies to accomplish the guaranteed learning. When curricula within the team are similar or related, the teachers can agree on the best approaches to engage students in the learning for guaranteed acquisition of a skill. For example, in construction and automotive trade programs of study, students are required to write budget estimates that include materials, parts, labor, taxes, and accurate computations. Perhaps students are measuring the cubic feet of gravel as a substrate for concrete, or estimating squares of siding including trim, or calculating the labor hours needed to complete a job, or setting rates that make a profit and are fair to the customer. These skills overlap across those CTE programs, as well as in courses of mathematics and finance. Once teachers identify the essential skills, they attack that essential learning as a team. If there is only one teacher on a team who teaches a particular field, that teacher would need to research the best strategies to affect the learning for each student in his or her program of study. Ideally, he or she would be able to collaborate with the other teachers regarding the research along with an examination of best practice for teaching and assessing the learning. When working on a team with colleagues who teach different courses, teams can focus on instructional practices, questioning techniques, scoring student work, instructional strategies, and routines.

When it comes to teacher learning, the following questions may prove helpful.

- **In what ways can the adults increase their learning to increase the rate of student learning?** Your team may want to set an agenda to include sharing specific instructional practices. Instructional-practice discussions could be focused on common essential skills within the same time frame, questioning techniques, and how to develop more refined and shorter cycle assessments to drive instruction and increase student learning.

- **How will CTE teachers identify and focus on what students will learn as a result of attending a specific CTE program of study?** For this question the team may want to discuss the differences they see between the attained and implemented curricula. They could also discuss methods for identifying essential learnings and any overlap that may exist in the different programs of study.

- **How might the instructional environment support learning the essential skills?** CTE teams can discuss ways to set up the instructional environment for teaching theoretical concepts and hands-on skills. Many CTE programs of study have lab settings and classroom settings. Teams can discuss seating arrangement strategies, grouping, examples of quality work, modeling academic and social behaviors, and so on.

- **How can CTE teachers ensure students are learning during instruction?** Teachers on the CTE team can discuss questioning techniques, opportunities for students to demonstrate their learning, ways to help struggling students, ways to challenge higher performing students, methods for conducting self- and peer-assessments, and so on.

A Collaborative Culture and Collective Responsibility

The second big idea of a PLC is collaborative culture and collective responsibility. These two components are inseparable in a highly effective team. Teams will need clarity on strategies to collaborate effectively, not only for job-alike teachers but also when the teachers on the team teach different programs of study. In CTE, a teacher may be on a team where no one teaches the same curriculum. We understand that ostensibly it isn't logical to collaborate on something that team members do not have in common, but there is an overwhelming logic in and need for collaboration. Finding commonalities—though especially complex when one or more CTE programs are involved—is possible.

As we mention in the introduction (page 4), once CTE team members are willing to acknowledge what they do not have in common and then shift the focus to what they do have in common, they are positioned to have very productive collaborative team meetings that will have incredible impact on student and adult learning. Each team member should independently study the meaning of professional collaboration and as a team agree on a team definition of *collaboration*. It may be a good starting point to consider this definition of collaborative teams: "the fundamental structure of a PLC is the collaborative teams of educators whose members work interdependently to achieve common goals for which members are mutually accountable" (DuFour et al., 2016, p. 12). We would like to highlight the three parts of this definition.

1. **Common goals:** To be a collaborative team, teachers must be able to identify a common goal they want to achieve. Depending on the size and structure of your team, there may be several different programs of study offered. Diversity of programs can lead to rich conversations but difficulty finding common content. If there are multiple building trades being taught, the collaborative team could agree on learning a process for completing a purchase order as a goal to achieve within a given time frame for all CTE students. With this approach the entire team could agree on a common assessment, a protocol to administer the assessment, how to score the assessment, and a goal for achievement based on the assessment results.

   If the team can't find a matching skill related specifically to their curricula, they could agree to have all students learn a skill that is considered valuable by the team, even if it is not specified by all curricula. With this approach, a team may focus their efforts on things like writing a résumé or letter of application for employment, calculating labor rates, budgeting for project materials, or other skills that will help students work and live independently. This could even include interpersonal skills like demonstrating a firm handshake with good eye contact and an introductory greeting.

2. **Interdependence:** Interdependence is necessary when one team member cannot accomplish the goal without his or her colleagues. For example, if a team guarantees that all CTE students will learn a particular skill (common goal), and some students do not learn the skill, the team needs to function interdependently to achieve the intended level of learning for all the team's students. There is a fundamental assumption that one team member does not possess all the skills that the team does collectively.

3. **Mutual accountability:** Once a skill is identified as essential, there must be mutual accountability by all team members to teach the skill to the students in a way that will have a level of effect on student learning which can be measured by the team's common assessment. When a team agrees on a skill and one of the team members goes back to his or her classroom and does not teach the agreed-on skill, the team will not be able to achieve their common goal. Without a common goal and common instructional practices, the team has little to hold themselves mutually accountable to. Being mutually accountable means teams are willing to professionally challenge and hold each other accountable to the team's expectations. Mutual accountability comes with a commitment to processes, outcomes, and one another. Commitment is a more desirable attribute of a team than compliance. Compliance usually comes when there are directives from above the team, while commitments come from within the team.

A Focus on Results

The third big idea is to work with a continuous and relentless focus on results. Focusing on the results of common assessments the team develops is one of the very powerful approaches to manage instruction and guide student learning. The team can use results of their assessments to gauge their level of effectiveness with student learning, examine best practices of teaching, and learn from each other about systems that affect learner outcomes. In addition to the common assessment results focused specifically on student learning, our CTE teams focus on results related to grade distribution, homework completion, behavior referrals, enrollment, tardiness, number of students being offered employment with benefits, and number of students being offered scholarships. While a student offered a scholarship may not ultimately enroll in the school that offered it, we know the program helped the student reach a level of learning at which postsecondary institutions are willing to compensate him or her.

To reinforce a focus on results, all teams need measurable goals. One way to approach this is through SMART goals. SMART goals are designed to be specific and strategically aligned to the larger organization goals, measurable, attainable, results oriented, and time bound. Following these guidelines assists teams in clarifying their goals and identifying when they have achieved their goals. SMART goals can be focused on most anything a team decides to improve on that can be measured within a certain time frame, such as essential learnings, certifications, employment offerings, and attendance. We will discuss SMART goals in more detail in chapter 6 (page 104).

As an example of a CTE program goal, in one of our schools, the automotive technology teacher had several goals for increased enrollment, amount of scholarships offered to students, and gainful employment opportunities in the industry. He and his students made posters showing all the scholarships available, which included monetary scholarships for tuition at postsecondary automotive programs and awards of tools and equipment for students accepting job offers at participating local dealerships. The posters displayed three years of historical data—so students could see that their opportunities were expanding—and goals for the current year. This teacher also developed relationships with local dealerships in order to understand their employment needs and partner with them to offer job shadowing, part-time work, and full-time employment after graduation. Over time, more and more dealerships wanted to get involved, further increasing opportunities for these students.

Other CTE teachers shared information about the number of students taking their courses and how many of those students went to postsecondary education or directly into a field of work related to the programs of study they had completed. Now picture that same information in the course catalog when students are selecting electives they want to take and how it might impact their decisions. With this approach, students and parents could see how CTE not only prepares students for college and careers, but actually helps them secure employment or enroll in postsecondary education. Better communication of the advantages of CTE programs of study can boost enrollment.

Once a CTE team develops a routine for determining what they have in common and measuring their effectiveness, the possibilities are endless. The team can concentrate on factors that demonstrate students' levels of learning and factors that interfere with or support student learning. In any case, effective collaboration embraces the second big idea (a collaborative culture and collective responsibility) with emphasis on the first big idea (a focus on learning) and using the third big idea (a focus on results) to determine the level of effectiveness and growth. Using the three big ideas as anchor vocabulary will help keep a team's efforts focused. Teams and individuals can use these ideas to assess team decisions. Does the decision embrace the three big ideas? If so, the decision may be more focused on learning; if not, the decision may be more grounded in someone's personal agenda. At any point, any stakeholder should feel empowered to say, "I need help seeing how our current efforts or conversation are falling under any of the three big ideas." When it becomes apparent the efforts are not focused on the priorities, using this language could help refocus valuable time and energy.

The Four Critical Questions

In addition to the three big ideas, four critical questions guide the work of a PLC. The authors of *Learning by Doing* (DuFour et al., 2016) emphasize the importance of focus: "The purpose of collaboration—to help more students achieve at higher levels—can only be accomplished if the professionals engaged in collaboration are focused on the *right work*" (p. 59). CTE programs play a valuable role in schools, providing students learning opportunities to build knowledge and skills that support success in college and careers. Although CTE programs of study tend to represent a diverse population of students with varying backgrounds, interests, skills, and abilities, the right work is the same: any CTE teacher will ensure *all* students learn at high levels in *all* classes. In complement, the diverse background of CTE teachers offers an impressive foundation to address this grand mission of learning for all students. Informed by the three big ideas, teams should focus their collaborative time on the four critical questions related to student learning. These questions are vital for CTE teachers and teams to address in a cyclical manner, repeatedly! The questions do not change, only the answers change as the year and curriculum progress. The following sections detail each question.

 These questions are vital for CTE teachers and teams to address in a cyclical manner, repeatedly!

What Is It We Want Our Students to Know and Be Able to Do?

The first critical question directs teams' attention toward learning requirements for students. In a PLC, we refer to learning requirements as *essential*. When we use the word essential in this book, we mean that when a team agrees on something, it is no longer up for debate. Throughout this book you may see the word *essential* followed by *standards*, *skills*, *learning targets*, and *success criteria*. In response to this question, a CTE teacher or team identifies essential learning targets, skills, or standards that would be considered non-negotiable for a student to learn.

Teams might also consider:

- What are the essential standards, learning targets, and enduring skills that CTE students will learn?
- How will the team sequence the curriculum for a concerted instructional effort?
- How will the team make decisions on what will qualify as essential or attained curricula?

How Will We Know Each Student Has Learned It?

The second critical question relates to assessment. In a PLC, assessments should be short, frequent, and part of the instructional process. In other words, assessment results should be used in a formative manner, to inform the instructional application and learning goals for the student and teacher. Whenever possible, teams should build assessments collaboratively with agreed-on expectations, scoring, protocols, and proficiency ratings. Student learning goals (in the format of SMART goals) should form the basis of assessments. Teachers can work together to identify these goals and monitor the progress of student learning based on the assessment results. Teams can start with the question, What are the common formative assessments our team will use during the learning process to assess students' growth toward achieving the essential standards, learning targets, or enduring skills?

How Will We Respond When Some Students Do Not Learn It?

Students learn in different ways and at different rates. For students who do not reach proficiency on the essential targets from initial instruction, teachers and teams must intervene to guarantee learning for all. Interventions must be *targeted*, *timely*, and *directive* (DuFour et al., 2016).

- **Targeted:** The intervention should be explicitly targeted to the specific skill the student is struggling to learn. Intervention should be more than general support like providing additional time or resources, and it should focus on one skill at a time as it aligns to the success criteria of the identified learning target.

- **Timely:** The intervention should be provided immediately following the assessment that identified the learning need. The longer the student has to wait for targeted support, the more difficult it will be to catch up. The team needs to determine a benchmark for timely responses. The shorter the time frame, the better the results will be for student learning.

- **Directive:** Intervention should be mandatory, not optional. The individual teacher does not have a choice about providing support to improve learning. The student cannot opt out of the support. The team should define expectations for intervention that they will all abide by.

Teams should discuss the question, What interventions will we use when reteaching individuals or small groups of students when they do not learn the essential standards, learning targets, or enduring skills?

How Will We Extend the Learning for Students Who Have Demonstrated Proficiency?

Students who achieve essential learning targets need opportunities to apply their knowledge and skills beyond the current curriculum. CTE curricula are rich, and students who demonstrate proficiency must receive opportunities to extend, enrich, challenge, and deepen their learning. Enrichment and extension must also be timely, project- and problem-based events. CTE teams should plan for the question, What extension or enrichment opportunities will we provide to students who demonstrate skills at proficiency levels and above?

It is important for teams to clarify what they will collaborate about when they meet. The four critical questions should be the primary focus of CTE collaborative team time. The questions should be discussed in the order listed (DuFour et al., 2016).

1. What is it we want our students to know and be able to do?
2. How will we know each student has learned it?
3. How will we respond when some students do not learn it?
4. How will we extend the learning for students who have demonstrated proficiency?

The questions are interconnected. As soon as teams feel confident they have addressed the first question, they should move on to the next. When the team resolves all questions for a set of essential learning outcomes, they should start the cycle again with question one for the next set of essential learning outcomes. This work is what guides the CTE team's instructional cycle.

Figure 1.1 illustrates embedding the four critical questions into routine practices. The cyclical process of addressing the four critical questions could occur over a week, two weeks, or perhaps a month's time. The time frame should not exceed four weeks to ensure that students needing additional support receive it in a timely fashion, and even four weeks is a long time for students to wait. The shorter the cycle, the timelier the feedback, which means more time to make thoughtful adjustments.

The Five Collaborative Outcomes for CTE Teams

A collaborative team might consist of all CTE teachers of the same or similar curriculum, or it might be one CTE teacher working with teachers of music, physical education, or other areas. Regardless, there are two key reasons CTE teachers need to collaborate within teams. The first reason is to ensure successful learning experiences for *all* students the team represents. The second reason is to provide job-embedded,

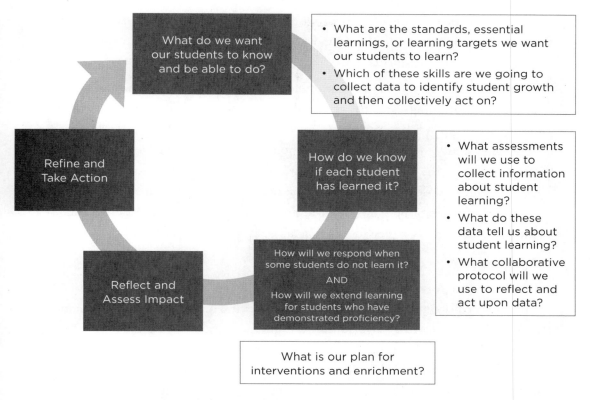

Figure 1.1: CTE-team instructional cycle.

peer-driven support for professional learning that supports the continuous growth of *all* teachers on the team. There are five outcomes for collaborative CTE teams that lead to success for *all* students and *all* teachers.

1. Common learning expectations

2. Common assessments

3. Collection of evidence

4. Critical analysis of the evidence

5. Action based on analysis

Common Learning Expectations

Having common learning expectations means teams identify their common denominators—the content, skills, or practices they share when addressing the first critical question, What is it we want our students to know and be able to do? Creating common learning expectations within teams where all teachers are CTE teachers appears to be an easier task to accomplish than for a team of teachers who represent different content areas. However, the first question is still important regardless of team members' content areas. A team must address the first question before they can respond to the second question, or there would be no content for which to develop assessments.

When the team is all CTE teachers, there is a better likelihood they will be able to find common learning outcomes across all their curricula: calculations, writing, formulas, and so on. When the membership of a team is mixed, such as one teacher each from CTE, music, art, and physical education, they may consider a learner outcome that will support the learning of all students, but not directly relate to their content. Examples for these learner outcomes might include time management, notetaking, keeping a calendar, or developing self-improvement goals. The list of valuable skills students could learn is endless, depending on the creativity and flexibility of the team.

Common Assessments

After teams agree on common denominators and common learning expectations, teams work collaboratively to address the second critical question, How will we know each student has learned it? To address this question, teams create common assessments that provide the team, the individual classroom teachers, and students with critical and targeted data that show what the students know and are able to do. In some cases, the data clarify support systems necessary for students. Even when team members teach different programs of study, they can identify skills and behaviors that can be assessed in common from teacher to teacher. Again, finding common denominators and agreeing on essential learning will come easier if you are teamed with other CTE teachers. In the case where you are the only one who teaches a subject, this work can still be achieved and will bring much needed clarity to students' essential learnings.

Collection of Evidence

Although CTE teachers tend to have a firm grasp on student learning within their own programs of study, no teacher or team should rely on intuition to make decisions about a student's knowledge, skill, or understanding of the content. Teams need to collect evidence of student learning through a variety of formative and summative assessments. Formative assessments are used to inform the teacher and student of the learning progress. Formative assessment data often have little to no impact on a student's grade. In contrast, a summative assessment often occurs at the end of an instructional cycle, unit, or grading period, and is used to assign the student a grade. Some teachers may refer to a summative assessment as a *summary* of the learning process and a formative assessment as part of or *for* the learning process. While creating assessments, the CTE team should be asking, "Will this assessment's data provide us the best evidence of student learning?"

Critical Analysis of the Evidence

Once a CTE team has collected evidence, the team must take time to examine it together and identify areas of success and areas for improvement. To critically analyze evidence of student learning in a safe and collaborative environment, CTE teams must establish protocols for predicting, reflecting, and taking action based on the data. Establishing a culture of collective inquiry, where teams ask themselves questions like, "What do these data tell us about student learning?" and "What do these data tell us about our teaching?" takes time and a commitment to the continual growth of the team.

> Some teachers may refer to a summative assessment as a *summary* of the learning process and a formative assessment as part of or *for* the learning process.

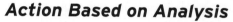

Action Based on Analysis

Learning by Doing is not only the title of *A Handbook for Professional Learning Communities at Work* (DuFour et al., 2016), but also the linchpin to successful collaborative CTE teams. CTE teachers must commit to learning by doing things together as they establish their team's culture of collaboration. This culture is especially important when addressing the third critical question (How will we respond when some students do not learn it?) and the fourth critical question (How will we extend the learning for students who have demonstrated proficiency?).

These questions are designed to directly respond to the data collected through common formative assessments. Many teams stall after they administer the assessment and review the results; they need to craft an action plan based on the analysis of results. When the team uses the results to identify students who need intervention, additional practice, or extension, they develop a team plan of action. Teams also act on the results to identify best practices in instruction and assessment. These tasks should not be the responsibility of one member of the team. When the team develops a plan, this plan includes all members of the team. They will learn by doing the work together.

Moving CTE Teams Past PLC Lite

CTE teams already have a full plate of responsibilities that not only include cultivating students' learning, but also completing daily tasks of maintaining labs, managing budgets, ordering supplies and tools, keeping tools and equipment clean and in safe working order, and organizing events such as national competitions with CTE youth organizations. All these tasks are important and should be addressed. However, for some CTE teams, these tasks overshadow their long-term goal of improving student learning. For your CTE team to make significant strides in ensuring students acquire content and skills, you must focus your collaborative team time on the three big ideas, four critical questions, and five collaborative CTE team outcomes. To accomplish these challenging yet impactful tasks, your team must establish a clear purpose that propels the team's existence, adhere to team norms, and align the team's work with the district mission and vision. For your teams to avoid falling into what is sometimes called *collaboration lite* or *PLC lite*, managerial conversations about calendars and coordinating should occur over email or other digital means of communication (DuFour, 2003). Consider distributing the guidelines shown in figure 1.2 to all team members as your team starts collaborating. This is a quick reference and should be referred to frequently, especially when new members join your team. As your team progresses, add more team-developed guidelines. This will help to define the culture of your team.

The Outcomes of CTE Team Collaboration	
Do This	**Don't Do This**
Design common learning expectations.	Organize or manage stuff.
Develop common assessments.	Talk about calendar items.
Collect evidence of student learning.	Complain about things with no action plan for resolution.
Critically analyze evidence in search of what will work better than in the past.	Hold onto beliefs that have no evidence of working today.
Take action—plan and implement student learning intervention and extension.	Put off action until the team agrees they have a flawless plan.
Discuss things the team can influence.	Have laborious discussions about things the team has no control over.
Argue over things that will improve student learning.	Argue to defend preferences or personal agendas.

Figure 1.2: Guidelines for a culture of collaboration.

To avoid falling into PLC lite, your team should assess your strengths and areas of need as an ongoing process. A team survey to guide this evaluation appears in appendix B (page 151). In addition to assessing the CTE teams' strengths and needs, another way to fend off PLC lite is to create a schedule of events for your team to execute. As your CTE team starts to put your plan of action together, making concrete decisions with a concise schedule of events to process will be critical. Timelines that include data reflection are powerful and necessary to successfully address student learning—hold yourself and your teammates accountable to see your plan through to the end. Be sure to include time for reflection with any action plan your team creates and adopts. Do not worry about perfection when it comes to such plans. No plan provides no opportunities to learn as a team. Even an imperfect plan offers many opportunities to reflect and learn together as you discover best curriculum, instructional, and assessment practices. Chapter 3 (page 49) and chapter 6 (page 108) will discuss scheduling and action planning in more detail.

Vital Action Steps for CTE Teams

Completing the following action items will help you put the ideas from this chapter into practice in your school.

- If misconceptions about CTE exist at your school, engage in team conversations to identify approaches to change any negative misconceptions by staff, students, or the community.

- Develop a shared vocabulary defining the three big ideas within CTE teams, what they are, and what they are not. A resource to guide this process appears in appendix B (page 150).

- Identify how your team will use the four critical questions to guide the work of your team.

- Draft a calendar with proposed dates for your team to implement the five collaborative outcomes for CTE teams.

- Identify hurdles your team might encounter when implementing PLC processes in the culture of your team. What steps might your team take to overcome these hurdles?

- When your team is ready, invite your administrator to a team meeting to offer suggestions about integrating CTE teachers and teams in the school's PLC process.

CHAPTER 2

Forming
Collaborative Teams

Being on a team without understanding what the team must accomplish and why all members must accomplish it is disingenuous to the second big idea of a PLC, a collaborative culture and collective responsibility. When members are not sure why their team exists or what their roles are on the team, it can cause them to be disconnected and operate from a sense of compliance rather than commitment. Worse yet, when members are new to the collaborative team concept, they may decide they prefer isolation, and "isolation is the enemy of improvement" (DuFour, Eaker, & DuFour, 2005, p. 141). This chapter discusses ways to avoid ambiguity and bring teams together, identify a futuristic picture, and create an enthusiastic, improvement-minded membership. Specifically, the following sections discuss establishing a CTE team structure that provides teachers opportunities for job-embedded professional learning, developing a clear purpose for your team, identifying the common denominators of the courses you represent, and aligning the CTE team vision to the school and district vision for student learning. These steps ensure the successful formation of CTE teams where all members feel supported and eager to learn together.

Establishing Teams

As a first step to productive CTE teams, key stakeholders must determine the kind of team structure that will be most beneficial in terms of providing teachers opportunities for job-embedded professional learning that produces the best results for all students their team represents. In the book *How to Develop PLCs for Singletons and Small Schools* (2015), Aaron Hansen describes four approaches to organizing teams. Depending on the intended student learning outcomes of the CTE team, any of these four options can provide the structure needed for purposeful collaboration

(DuFour et al., 2016; Hansen, 2015). In addition to these four structures, we propose a fifth option.

1. Vertical teams
2. Interdisciplinary teams
3. Singletons who support teams
4. Virtual teams
5. Blended teams

The following sections detail each structure.

Vertical Teams

A *vertical team* is a team of teachers who teach within the same career pathway, but do not teach the same courses. Career pathways tend to address similar skills and curricular standards but at different grade or skill levels. An example of a vertical CTE team in the finance career cluster might consist of educators who teach bookkeeping, accounting 1, accounting 2, and advanced accounting. A vertical CTE team in the agriculture, food, and natural resources cluster might include teachers of introduction to food and nutrition, food preparation, gourmet foods, and advanced gourmet foods.

Interdisciplinary Teams

An *interdisciplinary team* is a team of teachers who teach different content but work collaboratively toward common goals. This team structure is common in small schools that offer multiple singleton courses. Teachers collaborating within an interdisciplinary team might represent different pathways within one career cluster or entirely different career clusters. An example of an interdisciplinary team in a small school might be the agriculture teacher, building trades teacher, family and consumer sciences teacher, and business education teacher. In some cases, this team may include teachers from other elective areas, such as music, art, and so on. In all these examples, the interdisciplinary teams representing different content areas identify common content or skills they expect students to learn. Then, they work collaboratively to establish similar standards, learning targets, and criteria to indicate proficiency that will be communicated to the students.

Singletons Who Support Teams

A *singletons who support team* is a team of several teachers from a specific content area and one singleton CTE teacher. The role of the CTE teacher on this team is to support the goals of that team—even if the goal does not directly connect to his or her CTE program of study. An example of this team structure might be when a technology education teacher is a member of a science or mathematics team. Although the technology education teacher might not share the same learning targets as the science or mathematics teachers, the technology education teacher does teach students how to apply mathematics and scientific skills in a practical environment and can share his or her expertise to support that learning.

Virtual Teams

A *virtual team* is a team of teachers who work interdependently toward common goals but may not teach in the same building or even in the same district. CTE teachers are often the only ones teaching their content on that campus, so it is beneficial to find teammates with whom they share specific content at another school or district. The use of cloud storage and digital face-to-face technology makes it easy to share curriculum, instruction, and assessment practices with a job-alike partner at other schools. In this case, CTE teachers might also belong to teams within their own schools so they can contribute to and be part of the local school community.

Blended Teams

A *blended team* is a combination version of two or more of the other four team structures. It is "a group of diverse professionals with a common purpose, appreciation, and understanding, who work collaboratively towards common student learning goals" (Custable, 2013, pp. 7–8). Knowing that every school and every CTE program can be unique, a blended team is a practical team structure CTE teachers can use to work interdependently toward common student learning goals. An example of a blended team might be a group of singleton teachers who teach various levels or courses within the same career pathway. An arts, audiovisual technology, and communications pathway team might represent teachers who teach audiovisual production 1 and 2, photography 1 and 2, graphic design, and interactive media courses.

Defining a Clear CTE Team Purpose

In order for your teams to be high functioning and collaborative in the truest sense of the meaning, you must first identify a clear purpose with explicit commitments. Simply put, the team must define and understand why it exists. This is critical if teams are to meet the high demands of student learning. Having a purpose and clear commitments to that purpose seems to come easier for a team of science or English teachers, perhaps, because they have common curricula and may even teach the same grade levels or courses. However, for CTE teams this is often a new concept and a different set of expectations from what CTE teachers are accustomed to. The purpose of a team's existence can be much more difficult to define, and school leadership often does not expect this level of commitment from teams of multiple content areas. In extreme cases, singleton CTE teachers may get placed on random teams with no logical reason or clearly defined purpose and will end up attending meetings out of compliance and without commitment to the team's function.

We often find that teams of singleton teachers or those on teams from other content areas are members in name only; they usually lack direction and purpose, let alone have ground rules for how they should function as a team. These teams and teachers often become frustrated because there is no clear or agreed-on purpose for the team's existence. It might be even more frustrating for these same teachers if they don't believe they have anything in common to begin with. And if that is their perception, how would they even begin to agree on the team's purpose?

We see this frequently in our work when helping schools incorporate PLC processes in teams, especially among blended teams that include CTE and other singleton teachers. In many cases, a school leader either reads a book about PLC or attends a PLC conference and—perhaps with input from others or perhaps not—she develops a plan to assign all teachers to at least one curriculum team. Assigning teams usually goes smoothly for the core curricular areas. There are multiple teachers teaching the same course and often there are established essential skills (for example, from Common Core standards) that transcend grade levels (for example, English 9, 10, 11, and 12). The purpose and common goals of these teams are clear. However, in CTE and other elective or singleton curricula, the commonalities between programs of study that comprise a team are not always as salient.

It is imperative that all teams have absolute clarity of their purpose and the expected outcomes from their team's collaborative work. There are several methods to developing a purpose for teams, as well as approaches to avoid when establishing teams that include CTE or other singleton teachers.

When working with teams to create a statement of purpose, have each member write one sentence defining the primary purpose of the CTE team's existence. Next, discuss each of the responses, write them on chart paper, look for commonalities, and collaboratively clarify the team's purpose. The CTE team would then include their resulting purpose statement on the top of their team meeting agendas and refer to it at the beginning of each team meeting. For example, the CTE and fine arts team at Monticello Middle School in Monticello, Arkansas, defined their purpose as follows:

"The purpose of the Fine Arts and Business Ed team is to collaborate and analyze data to direct our instruction so our students may achieve high levels of learning" (K. Rodriguez, personal communication, February 22, 2020). This team worked collaboratively to establish this purpose and, more important, committed to each other that they will work interdependently to live by this purpose. We strongly discourage shortcutting this process by someone creating a purpose for the team; that approach will take the team backward into compliance, not commitment.

For teams to build on this type of clarity about their purpose, they must also identify what they have in common regarding skills, content, and behaviors that students will learn—the team's common denominators.

Identifying Team Common Denominators

While the three big ideas are an essential foundation for teams, they can feel overwhelming to CTE teams. To focus their work, teams need to find their *common denominators*. Common denominators are content, skills, and behavior expectations that all team members share. In the beginning of collaborative attempts, it might seem impossible to find anything that the unique CTE pathways have in common. What is shared between agriculture education, business education, family and consumer sciences, technology education, and health sciences? As mentioned previously, most CTE teachers are singletons in their programs and may even teach multiple singleton classes. Whether a CTE team is vertical, interdisciplinary, or blended, teachers need to identify their common denominators. Once CTE teams identify their common denominators, they will be able to engage in meaningful and productive collaborative practices that will advance the learning of all CTE students.

CTE teams should begin this identification process by engaging in conversations with their teammates. Even though specific content is not usually common across CTE programs of study, the skills taught to students often are. Teams of CTE teachers can reflect on the question, What common skills might you have among the programs of study? It is a simple and direct question that builds a foundation for teachers to list skills they expect students to learn from the programs of study the team represents. Once teachers move past looking at their differences, they will see there are many common skills between their programs of study. When we have these conversations with CTE teams, we find the commonalities for student learning are often in one or more of the following skills.

- Literacy
- Mathematics
- Measurement
- Financial literacy

- Communication
- Employability
- Vocabulary
- Writing
- Self-presentation
- Teamwork and collaboration
- Leadership
- Problem solving
- Technology

Some programs of study may share more of these skills than others. If your team cannot identify any connection from the previous list, you should create your own list of shared specific skills. In addition, the team should take the same approach with broad transferable skills, which could include employability and 21st century skills.

Developing a Mission and Vision

In our work with CTE teams, we find that most have little experience establishing a mission and vision for their work. Without the clarity that a mission and vision provide, CTE teams can easily get derailed from their student learning goals. To stay on track, CTE teams need to be clear on what they want to achieve and how their efforts align with the efforts of the school and district.

In some cases, schools and districts have a mission that communicates the purpose of the organization and guides the day-to-day operations that staff carry out to be successful. Others have a vision that clarifies who or what the organization is striving to become. Still others have both a mission and a vision in place to achieve their long-term goals. If your school or district has an established mission or vision, or both, your team should develop a set of commitments that aligns with it. If by chance your district does not have either a mission or vision, then you should create your own.

To accomplish this important task of developing a team mission and vision, you need to develop an understanding of what you want to achieve as a team, especially how it relates to student learning. DuFour and his colleagues (2016) discuss how the mission statement answers the question, "Why do we exist?" (p. 39). It states the fundamental purpose of the team and can be used to prioritize team action steps and goals. The vision is long term—what you hope to eventually become.

A vision needs to be compelling yet realistic; it provides direction for the district, school, and team's efforts. It communicates to all stakeholders what can be expected of the district, school, and teams in the school. For example, the mission of Adlai E. Stevenson High School is "Success for Every Student." This mission permeates the entire organization, including CTE teams, making it a priority to ensure all students learn at high levels every day. The mission provides guidance for the operations that are carried out in the five categories of the school's vision statement: curriculum; equity, access, and inclusivity; professional learning community; culture for learning; and community engagement (Stevenson High School, n.d.). Each of these categories addresses an important aspect of the school as it relates to ensuring success for every student. At Stevenson, the day-to-day work is making it a priority for students to be successful learners. All stakeholders are active participants to ensure the mission and vision become a reality.

Joyce Kilmer Middle School's vision is "We will be the top-performing middle school in the state within the next five years;" the mission is "Kilmer Cougars dare to excel." Everyone on campus knows where the school stands regarding its performance rating from the state. They are confident they know what it takes to achieve their mission and vision. The mission and vision permeate the school: they display posters and sing chants about their quest to rise to the top. This quest includes clarifying their essentials, checking for understanding, helping struggling students, and extending learning for excelling students.

Some schools spend months engaging all staff in establishing a mission and vision. Figure 2.1 presents a simpler approach; these steps might occur during a half-day staff meeting at the beginning of the year or when first establishing a CTE team.

Mission Development	Number of People	Time
In small groups, review mission statements from other schools and organizations to gain ideas for your own mission statement.	Groups of 4 or fewer	30 min
Give all members an index card and ask them to write what they believe the mission statement should be.	1	5 min
Each member connects with one other member in the room. They discuss both statements and either agree on one, merge the two, or create a new draft. The result must fit on one side of an index card.	2	5 min
Repeat the above process, doubling the number of people each time.	4	5 min
Repeat the above process, doubling the number of people each time.	8	5 min
Repeat the above process, doubling the number of people each time.	16	5 min

Figure 2.1: Vision and mission development.

continued →

Repeat these steps until all members have been involved. Within about an hour of this activity, a faculty of 128 people could have a first draft of a mission statement. Once all members have had a chance to contribute, there will be a draft of the mission statement to reference in the creation of a vision statement.

Post the rough draft of the mission and assign a subcommittee to wordsmith the statement. This might be done online over the next few weeks where everyone can see the work.

Vision Development	Number of People	Time
Give all members an index card and ask them to write a one-line news flash about their school they would be proud to see within the next five years.	1	5 min
Each member connects with one other member in the room. They discuss both news headlines and either agree on one, merge the two, or create a new draft. The result must fit on one side of an index card.	2	5 min
Repeat the above process, doubling the number of people each time.	4	5 min
Repeat the above process, doubling the number of people each time.	8	5 min
Repeat the above process, doubling the number of people each time.	16	5 min

Repeat these steps until all members have been involved. Depending on the size of the faculty or team, you may want to consolidate the statements or perhaps retain all of them for later reference when developing action plans to address this vision. Again, give these statements to a subcommittee to wordsmith a final vision statement.

Alignment With the School and District

CTE teams should align their efforts to the big-picture goals of the school. If the school does not have a mission or vision, or the existing mission and vision do not prioritize student learning, CTE teams should create their own. Once CTE teams align to the district and school mission and vision, they should establish a process to keep themselves on track. During team discussions, any member of the team can and should ask how the team's current efforts are aligned with their vision, mission, and purpose. In some situations, the work or conversations may not be aligned. Examples of distractions could include organizing materials, stressing over lack of parent involvement, complaining about other teachers or administrators, or swapping stories. In cases like these, the team should be able to openly acknowledge the deviation and refocus their efforts. This redirection is easiest if the mission, vision, and purpose were developed collaboratively. Deviations are normal, but high performing CTE teams assess and realign their efforts seamlessly.

Figure 2.2 shows an example of aligned visions and missions for a district, school, and CTE team. While these are only examples and may not work for every team, we do advocate learning together to understand your school and district mission and vision, and, as a team, tailoring your own vision to motivate learning and continued growth. For some of the schools we have worked in, the vision for each team is included in the school improvement plan. These schools also craft an action plan to achieve their stated vision.

District Mission	We inspire students to meet high academic and life standards to be responsible citizens.
School Mission	We excel for our students every day.
CTE Team Mission	We stay on the cutting edge of workforce needs and skills.
District Vision	All students will be ready for college, career, and life.
School Vision	All students will earn a diploma on time and be accepted for college or employment upon graduation.
CTE Team Vision	All CTE students will demonstrate skills necessary for employment with benefits.

Figure 2.2: Mission and vision alignment.

Action Plans

Creating the mission and vision of the team is easy compared to making them a reality. To live the mission and achieve the vision, the real work of a CTE team is in the action plan. A plan of action describes specific team activities and is a critical component of achieving the vision. In fact, there must be some method of developing not just a plan, but multiple plans of action that align to achieving the vision. Action plans can seem overwhelming at times because they involve many moving parts. Breaking the overall plan down into mini-plans can be helpful to bring clarity on roles of the membership, timelines, and needed materials. Plan on several small action steps that a team can monitor and celebrate the wins along the way.

All teams should record their action plans. They are great for team reflection, they can be used to celebrate accomplishments, and they can serve as documentation of all the hard work your team does. The action-plan template in figure 2.3 (page 40) works well to document a team's action steps necessary to achieve the plan. This allows the team to work together on record keeping.

Team Name: CTE		Vision: All CTE students will demonstrate skills necessary for employment with benefits.						Academic Year: This year
Team work plans	Data sources	Status (continued or new)	Person or persons responsible	Professional learning	Materials needed	Timeline	Parent or community involvement	Evidence of completion
Develop and send a survey focused on employability skills to the employers who hire most of our students. The survey will include skills outlined in the Employability Skills Framework.	Team-developed survey results for this year and the results from last year's survey	C	Team Lead will be point but this will require input from all CTE teachers.	None at this time	Past surveys	Create the survey in the spring. Retrieve the survey and tally the results before the summer break. August: Develop a plan for teaching the skills throughout the year.	Local employers	Completed surveys Tallied results of the surveys Lesson plans based on the results

Team work plans: What specific actions will be taken?

Data sources: What data will be used to determine the effectiveness of the plan?

Status: C = Continued effort from previous months or years

Status: N = New plan of action

Person or persons responsible: Who will be a point person for this work plan? This does not need to be the person or persons that will do all the work, but they need to have knowledge of the team's efforts.

Professional learning: What learning is required for the team to address this plan? What might be possible professional learning opportunities? Try to plan as much professional learning to be completed "in house" as possible, and embed the professional development in the typical school calendar as much as possible (no money needed).

Materials needed: What materials and resources does the team need to complete the plan?

Timeline: What is the timeline for the plan? The shorter the timeline, the quicker the team can experience a celebration. Identify quarterly or shorter timelines.

Parent or community involvement: Do you or should you have parent or community involvement? It is great when parents and other community members are involved. However, since they do not work with us daily, it can be a risk depending on their level of involvement.

Evidence of completion: What is the evidence the team will provide or demonstrate to show growth or achievement?

Figure 2.3: Action-plan template.

Vital Action Steps for CTE Teams

Completing the following action items will help you put the ideas from this chapter into practice in your school.

- Offer to be on the master schedule team. Explain that you are interested in helping and finding ways to integrate CTE with the PLC practices.

- Locate model PLC schools at www.allthingsplc.info and read their PLC stories to see if they have included CTE; if so, examine any practices that could fit with your CTE team.

- Evaluate possible team configurations at your school and determine which structure will best serve student learning. Make it your priority to organize that configuration.

- Establish a clear purpose for your team; include a date of creation and the membership involved. Revisit the purpose frequently and revise it each year if necessary or when a new member joins the team.

- Identify as many common denominators as possible that are represented on your team.

- Align your team's goals to the district mission and vision.

- Develop an action plan to guide making the mission and vision a reality.

CHAPTER 3

Setting Up the Logistics of Teamwork

Once the team has formed and agreed on a shared purpose aligned to the mission and vision, they will need to work out the logistics. Team logistics include norms and expectations for how members will work together, the tools they will use, and commitments to their meeting schedules. These self-imposed rules keep the team on track throughout the year. Teaming logistics are especially powerful when the team members are involved in the creation process because that brings a higher level of dedication and commitment from all involved. All team members should participate in the development of these logistics and follow them during collaborative time and even outside team meetings. With a high level of commitment, the team can weather the storms they will encounter in their journey: "Effective teams do not settle for 'sorta' agreements; they identify the very specific commitments members have made to each other" (DuFour et al., 2016, p. 72).

In addition, when teams define their own logistics, it is very helpful for the supervising administrator. Since some supervisors will not have experience in CTE or other singleton curricular areas, they may not know how to support the team. However, if the team norms and expectations are clear and concise, a supervisor will know what to expect in team meetings and even in team members' classrooms. When administrators have access to the team-developed logistics, it is easier for them to identify what to promote and protect for the team. Commitment is always preferred over compliance, but there may be occasions where you need a supervisor's support to hold certain team members accountable to the team's commitments. To get that support, be concise about the commitments the team has made.

This chapter provides strategies for a team to define their practices that will lead to achieving their vision: tight and loose expectations, team meeting norms, a cycle of team meeting topics, agendas and record keeping strategies, and descriptions of the roles of team members.

Tight and Loose Expectations

In a PLC, there are certain universal expectations that all stakeholders must adhere to—these are the *tight* elements of the PLC process. At the same time, teachers are empowered to use their professional judgment and make decisions that will benefit their students' learning—reflecting the *loose* elements of the process (DuFour et al., 2016). CTE teams need to reach agreements on what they consider tight and loose. We define *tight* as non-negotiable, not up for question or discussion in a school or on a team. These elements require a high level of commitment and perhaps compliance from each team member. We define *loose* as presenting opportunities for teams or team members to be creative and have some autonomy. This autonomy can be in the processes, meetings, or in their classrooms. Furthermore, the word *and* is critical here: teams should avoid over-reliance on the notion of *or* (as in tight *or* loose). Teams and individual teachers sometimes mistakenly approach this concept as tight *or* loose, which would be a lot like ordering sweet-*or*-sour chicken from a Chinese restaurant. More often, a topic has aspects that are tight and other aspects that are loose. Tight and loose examples for CTE teams may include the following.

- **Team norms**
  - Tight: Teams must have and live by their norms.
  - Loose: Each team can identify their own meeting norms.

- **Use of student learning data**
  - Tight: Teams must collect and reflect on student learning data as a team to inform decisions.
  - Loose: Each team can decide which data they collect to inform their decisions.

- **Essential learning targets**
  - Tight: The team establishes a set of essential learning targets that all students will learn before the end of the course.
  - Loose: Each teacher decides on his or her own instructional approach to use in the classroom to ensure students learn the content.

- **Students arriving late to class**
  - Tight: Teams will enforce the school tardy policy.
  - Loose: Teachers can employ different instructional strategies to address students arriving late to their classes.

Team Meeting Norms

One important logistical step is to establish CTE collaborative team meeting norms. Teams may refer to norms as commitments, rules, or expectations. Regardless of what they are called, they need to be clear, concise, and focused on behaviors and processes. Developing and committing to team norms are non-negotiable expectations for all collaborative teams who want to have a positive and lasting impact on student learning. As Buffum and his colleagues (2018) assert, "We cannot overemphasize the importance of setting team norms—or collective commitments—to guide professional behavior while collaborating" (p. 72).

Norms do more than just help the team run their meetings efficiently and effectively. When norms are well written and focused on the needs of the team, they can help the team avoid the five dysfunctions of teams identified by Patrick Lencioni (2002):

1.   Inattention to results

2.   Avoidance of accountability

3.   Lack of commitment

4.   Fear of conflict

5.   Absence of trust

These factors all contribute to a team becoming dysfunctional. With the variables in CTE course content and lack of commonality among the team, any of the five dysfunctions can surface quickly. CTE teams should proactively avoid the dysfunctions, rather than deal with them after they surface. For example, to avoid fear of conflict, it would be helpful to have a norm that suggests the team is open to constructive conflict. This norm might be phrased, "We will embrace constructive conflict focused on what's best for student learning." To avoid inattention to results or avoidance of accountability, a team norm could be "We will consistently use results to validate our strategies and efforts" or "We will use SMART goals to determine and highlight our growth." A norm to avoid lack of commitment might sound like, "We will carry out all team agreements in our separate classrooms as appropriate," or "We will keep all conversations focused on items of the agenda."

Discounting the application and value of team norms can be catastrophic for your team. Developing norms should be a routine for any team, including CTE teams. During the norm-development process, some team members may suggest they don't need norms to work interdependently. These types of members usually state that the team is already cohesive and rarely argues about how to conduct business. In such a situation, your team should review the details of how its last difficult decision was processed. Did they already have an agreement on how to conduct the meeting? Was the topic on the agenda? Did all parties participate in the decision? Did all parties fully support and commit to the decision? If the answer to any of these questions is *no*, your team needs team meeting norms, and you may also be able to use those answers to your review as examples of why.

Teams usually have no problem reaching consensus on administrative items such as collecting field trip permission forms, distributing and collecting federal aid forms, coordinating the use of the computer labs and equipment, or nominating students for the monthly recognition program. However, as CTE teams begin to make decisions—difficult and new decisions that often have complex and personal roots—about creating common assessments, administering assessments, allowing make-up assignments, grading policies, comparing data, and discussing changes in their daily teaching practices, the team cohesiveness around these issues can be challenging. These discussions will be new for most CTE teams, and the commitments to follow these types of decisions will be cause for change in one's personal classroom practice. As a team strives to effect higher levels of student learning, norms will be necessary to guide these pivotal and potentially charged conversations. Establishing norms is beneficial to all members of the CTE team.

Norms should be developed to keep the team's energy focused, to provide processes to reach agreements, and to address a breach of the norms. CTE teams should be empowered to customize norms to meet their unique needs. Some teams will need norms more focused on behaviors while other teams need norms to focus on processes, and some teams will need both. For example, the team may establish norms such as the following.

- **Behavioral norms** focus on the behaviors of the members.
  - We will keep all conversations focused on agenda items.
  - We will respect and accept suggestions of others with an open mind.
  - We will avoid monopolizing the meeting with one speaker.
  - We will be open to new ideas.
- **Process norms** address the operations of team meetings.
  - We will have agendas and notes for all meetings.
  - We will deliver our team agenda twenty-four hours before the team meeting.
  - We will end all meetings with action plans to carry us to the next meeting.
  - We will start and end our meetings on time.

- **Breach norms** address violations of the team's norms.
  - All members will use a hand signal to indicate there is a violation of the team's norms. Examples may include pointing, waving, thumbs up, clapping, or even touching your nose with your index finger.
  - We will use a visual and auditory cue when a team norm is violated.
  - We will nudge the person to our right each time a team norm is violated.
  - We will say the word *norm* when a team norm is violated.

These are only examples. The norms themselves are not as important as the fact that they are developed by the team and each member is committed to the norms of the team. For some teams, this work will come easily, but others will have a more challenging experience, depending on the personality types of the members. When a team starts to develop their norms, they need to keep a record of the norms. This record becomes an artifact of the team's work; it is a resource the team can reference as frequently as necessary. Figure 3.1 is an example of what the norm record could look like after the team has processed through the following steps.

Team: Business Education	
Programs of study taught by team members: Introduction to Business, Business Applications, Accounting 1 and 2, Advanced Accounting, Marketing, Entrepreneurship, Business Law, Investment Management, Personal Finance	
Team members and their assigned roles: Jason (Facilitator), Jackie (Note Taker), Joe (Timekeeper), Taylor (Materials Clerk), Jen, Beth	
Positive Meeting Details	**Negative Meeting Details**
Everyone's voice is heard.	Some members dominate the conversation, while others might be disengaged.
There is a focus for the meeting.	There is no meeting agenda or plan.
Members are prepared and present.	Collective consensus is not built.
Someone takes notes and summarizes at the conclusion of the meeting.	Meeting conversations are about teacher needs rather than student learning needs.
Ways to Address a Breach of Norms	
We will yell *squirrel* when our conversations begin to go off topic.	
We will acknowledge our breach and respectfully address it as a team.	
Our Team Norms and Date of Agreement: September 6	

Figure 3.1: Sample business education team norms.   continued →

We will have a collaboration guide for each meeting.
We will be prepared and present for our team meetings.
We will listen and think from diverse perspectives.
We will support the work of our teammates and their students.
We will have and meet our established due dates.
We will use our devices for professional use only.

Visit **go.SolutionTree.com/PLCbooks** *for a free reproducible version of this figure.*

When working through this template for team norms, team members should first work individually and then discuss with the whole team to ensure all voices are heard before making final decisions and commitments. Use the following six steps to complete the collection tool and draft team norms.

1. In the section Positive Meeting Details, team members list things about meetings they participated in in the past that ran smoothly, seemed to be a good use of time, and resulted in a tangible outcome.

2. In the section Negative Meeting Details, team members reflect on and list the characteristics of a team meeting they attended that they felt did not run smoothly and was not a good use of their time.

3. In the section Ways to Address a Breach of Norms, team members list their suggestions on ways to address a breach of norms during a team meeting. The methods must be doable by any member, can be fun, but must be respectful of all members.

4. On a separate piece of paper, draft proposed team norms for your team. These norms should protect things team members like and address things they don't like about team meetings. Hold a vote or build consensus to decide on a final set of norms. Norms should help keep the team focused on issues of student learning and professional teacher growth.

5. In the section Our Team Norms and Date of Agreement, list the norms your team has decided on and date the agreement. Consider having all members sign the document. This document will serve as your written commitment.

6. Briefly revisit the team norms at the beginning of each meeting.

A Cycle of Team Meeting Topics

Another key logistical concern is when to meet and what to meet about. We recommend setting a schedule of recurring meetings and a cycle of meeting topics. Finding time for meetings is very difficult if the school leadership does not wholeheartedly support CTE team meetings and collaborative work. The administration must make it a priority to provide time during the contract day for collaboration if all members are expected to attend and participate. While some skeptics claim that there's just no way to find time for collaboration in their master schedules, many schools have figured out how to designate time in their daily schedules.

Providing time for collaboration can be done in many ways if the school is willing to get creative. Renee Smith-Faulkner, associate superintendent for Castleberry Independent School District in Texas, shares how her district provides time for the CTE teachers to collaborate (personal communication, June 23, 2019). The CTE teachers in Castleberry ISD do not have a common planning period built into the master schedule; they do not have to give up their lunch period to collaborate or get additional pay for time before or after the contract day. Instead, Castleberry ISD teachers took a no-cost and very clever approach. During a specific period of the day, the social studies, mathematics, English, or science teachers teach CTE students, which allows the CTE teachers time to collaborate. In doing so, the academic teachers take advantage of this additional time with the CTE students to reinforce required core academic content. While this approach increases the amount of time CTE students receive direct instruction from certified core academic teachers, it doesn't involve pull-outs from other classes, and is all being done to increase the levels of student learning. Smith-Faulkner specifically mentions the teacher-driven nature of the effort, supported but not directed by the administration. Visit www.allthingsplc.info/plc-locator/us to learn more about schools that have created time for job-embedded collaboration.

With time allocated, team members should identify all dates and times for their team meetings with as much advance notice as possible. All team members should put these appointments on their calendars and avoid conflicts with the dates. We know this sounds very basic, but how many meetings have you attended where a member doesn't show because of a conflict or because he or she claimed not to know the meeting was scheduled for that day? If everyone puts the dates in their calendars in advance, the team will find it is much easier to cancel a meeting when appropriate than to find a mutual time to meet after the year has started.

The next step is to identify what the team will work on at each meeting. In many cases, the leadership doesn't offer guidance to the CTE team regarding topics to address, so it is up to the team itself. The cycle of meeting topics will vary based on the number and frequency of meetings a team has scheduled. If your team is fortunate enough to have a common period or block to meet each week, the topics in figure 3.2 would keep the team focused on the right work in a four-week cycle. Other meetings could be scheduled as well, and in many cases a team may have other items to add to their schedule.

	Topic for the Team to Focus On
Week One	Agree on essential skills for the following month.
Week Two	Create common assessment questions aligned to the team's essential skills for next month and create the assessment.
Week Three	Discuss students and strategize on systems of support for this month's essential skills.
Week Four	Compare and discuss this month's common assessment results. Identify students for support and acceleration; get students scheduled in support sessions.

Figure 3.2: Team meeting topics—weekly meeting schedule.

This schedule focuses on the four critical questions of a PLC. For the first meeting, each team member could bring one or two skills students should learn the following month. During the meeting, the team would consider each member's contributions and agree to focus on specific skills as a team. Teams should agree on at least one skill for a four-week or shorter period; any number is fine as long as the team decides on it. For the second meeting of the cycle, each team member could come prepared with two to five assessment questions they would like to contribute to the team's common assessment. The team would review all the questions and as a team agree on the questions to use on their common assessment. The third meeting is to discuss concerns about providing instructional support to students as they learn the current month's skills. Finally, in the last meeting of the month, the team would share and discuss the results of the team-developed common assessment. Next month, the team would start the cycle again. If your team meets bi-weekly, try combining the first two topics of figure 3.2 for the first meeting and the last two topics for the second meeting. Please note that team members come to each meeting prepared and with something to contribute. Even with highly efficient teams, these tasks would be very difficult to accomplish during a forty-five- or ninety-minute meeting if the members didn't come prepared, which is why some work needs to be accomplished independently. Members of high-performing teams function as a team even in between meetings.

Some schools—particularly high schools—only provide time for CTE teams to meet on a monthly basis. These teams are often allocated additional time to meet in the beginning of the year and the end of the year. Some teams have additional collaboration time around the middle of the year. If your team is scheduled to meet on a monthly basis and perhaps on a couple of professional development days, the schedule could look something like the one in figure 3.3. The more the team can do during the beginning of the year, the easier it is to get started with a replicable cycle of events. It would be best if the team could work ahead by a month or more in identifying essential skills and creating their common assessments. Creating assessments before instruction starts is a critical step to the instructional planning, and we recommend declaring that rule as a non-negotiable expectation for all teachers and teams. This way the members will have clarity of what and how the student must learn and demonstrate their learning. A team could start a new cycle anytime during the year and could start the cycle focusing on the month ahead or two months ahead. Don't wait for a new year to start the process.

> Members of high-performing teams function as a team even in between meetings.

CTE Monthly Team Meeting Schedule	
August **Year 1**	Develop the team's mission, vision, purpose, and team meeting norms. Identify skills for September and October.
September	Agree on assessment questions for September and October skills. Agree on skills for November.
October	Agree on assessment questions for November. Agree on skills for December. Analyze assessment results.
November	Agree on assessment questions for December. Agree on skills for January. Analyze assessment results. Schedule students into support sessions.

Figure 3.3: Team meeting topics—monthly meeting schedule.

continued →

December	Agree on assessment questions for January.
	Agree on skills for February.
	Analyze assessment results.
	Schedule students into support sessions.
January Professional Day	Review the progress of the team.
	Develop new or refined goals.
	Review the team norms for continued applicability.
	Study instructional strategies.
January	Agree on assessment questions for February.
	Agree on skills for March.
	Analyze assessment results.
	Schedule students into support sessions.
February	Agree on assessment questions for March.
	Agree on skills for April.
	Analyze assessment results.
	Schedule students into support sessions.
March	Agree on assessment questions for April.
	Agree on skills for May.
	Analyze assessment results.
	Schedule students into support sessions.
April	Agree on assessment questions for May.
	Agree on skills for June.
	Analyze assessment results.
	Schedule students into support sessions.
May	Agree on assessment questions for June.
	Agree on skills for September.
	Analyze assessment results.
	Schedule students into support sessions.
June	Agree on assessment questions for September.
	Analyze assessment results.
	Schedule students into support sessions.
August Year 2	Develop and refine the team's mission, vision, purpose, and team meeting norms.
	Identify skills for October.

*Visit **go.SolutionTree.com/PLCbooks** for a free reproducible version of this figure.*

It goes without saying that approaching the team cycle as suggested will be more work in the beginning; however, if the work starts in the beginning of the year, by October the team is on a very reasonable cycle of team meeting topics. Another approach could be starting one or two months out—in August the team would set the skill focus for October, and then build the relevant common assessment in September. They would cycle forward each month from that point. These two models are only examples. Regardless of what schedule you set up, it will be better

High-performing teams shift their focus to future goals at the end of the school year.

than a random approach to the team meetings all year long. Additionally, be sure to note how the team's focus shifts to the following year during the last two months of the school year. High-performing teams shift their focus to future goals at the end of the school year. Rather than just shutting down, they incorporate sustainability efforts for the following year.

This is challenging work, especially when you are just starting out. However, if your team's new processes include a cycle of team meeting topics like the ones in figure 3.2 (page 50) and 3.3 (page 51), the team will have clarity about what it needs to do, and it will be something that can be shared with other teacher teams across campus. If your team struggles to sufficiently address important topics in the time provided by the school, consider scheduling additional collaborative meetings. We have found that when teams want to meet more often than the school expects, the membership is usually able to find a mutually agreeable time. If the team decides to identify additional time for meetings, it is advisable to keep the meeting times during the contract day. If your team asks for additional time with compensation, it will be helpful to inform the administration what your team will accomplish during that time.

Agendas and Record Keeping

Documenting collaboration is key if a team wants to repeat its success or avoid repeating mistakes or challenges. Record keeping shows trends and captures action plans, goals, and the progress of the team. A firm rule in our own schools is: if it is important enough to collaborate about, then it must be important enough to keep records. Well-kept records will provide the details of what took place in a meeting, as well as clear action plans that carry the team from one meeting to the next.

If it is important enough to collaborate about, then it must be important enough to keep records.

Agendas and records are another element that has both tight and loose facets. Requiring a team to use an agenda is a tight (mandatory) expectation. Allowing the team members to design their agenda format is a loose approach. Take a balanced tight-loose approach to records. Convince the team to compile clear notes of each meeting (including action plans) rather than telling them to take overly detailed minutes. Minutes can be seen as overkill while notes have a softer tone. Agendas and notes should not be cumbersome chores. The simpler the process, the more likely that team members will follow the process with fidelity. If your team is not keeping a record of their team meetings, an agenda like the one in figure 3.4 will be helpful.

Our Team Purpose Is . . .	
Our Team Norms Are . . .	**Our Meeting Date, Time, and Location Are . . .**
Our SMART Goal Is . . .	
Our Team's Common Essential Skills Are . . .	
Our Common Formative Assessments Are . . .	
Assessment name	Assessment timeline
Data Reflection	
Protocols	Data reflection timeline

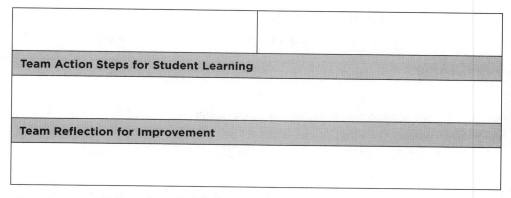

Figure 3.4: CTE team collaboration guide.

*Visit **go.SolutionTree.com/PLCbooks** for a free reproducible version of this figure.*

With this agenda, a team should create a template and prepopulate the areas that do not change, such as team purpose and team norms. The other topics in shaded lines are the agenda items for discussion during the meeting, and the white space allows teachers to record notes, outcomes, and decisions. The team might not discuss all the topics in one meeting; to help teachers arrive prepared, the team could write the meeting date by the topic to indicate when the team will address different topics. Some teams create agendas as online documents and include hyperlinks to other documents, such as that month's essential skills or assessments. To help streamline the team's process, we recommend using one document for this record keeping. The team starts with an electronic agenda and captures notes in the same document to consolidate information and avoid having many separate files.

Roles of Team Members

After teams establish the norms that will support their work, they need to determine and assign roles and responsibilities for conducting the business of the team meeting. Assigning roles spreads out the work of the team while keeping everyone invested in achieving their collaborative goals. Although each team may have specific needs that require unique roles, we find the following roles help keep CTE teams focused.

Team Leader

The team leader is the teacher who is responsible for facilitating team conversations to reach a collaborative agreement about the purpose of the team. The team leader would also be responsible for setting the team's meeting schedule and topics and maintaining and prioritizing agenda items. In addition, the team leader serves as the liaison between the team and the school's administration to communicate information and submit required paperwork. If you or your team are not comfortable with the title *team leader*, you might refer to this position as *point person* or similar.

Facilitator

The facilitator is the teacher assigned to ensure all voices are heard and the conversation sticks to the agenda. Whether the team is sharing instructional best practices, developing common formative assessments, or reflecting on student learning data, the facilitator's job is to help the team stay focused, make decisions, and take action. Collaboration protocols are extremely useful for keeping teams on task. As CTE teams become more seasoned, the role of facilitator should get easier.

Note Taker

The note taker's role is to log all critical points of the team conversations and decisions. Documenting meetings will serve to archive, clarify, and communicate the work of the team. Digital tools such as Google Docs can be useful for storing and sharing notes, especially when formal meetings are not frequent. Using online documents also makes it easier for a member to catch up if he or she was absent or to contribute to the discussion even when unable to physically attend the meeting.

Meeting Pacer

Regular face-to-face collaboration time to discuss teaching and learning is a gift that CTE teachers do not want to waste. The pacer is the team member who watches the time to keep the team on track to meet its goals. When establishing team norms, the team members should identify how they want the pacer to operate when the team gets off task. One silly but effective approach is to identify a word like *squirrel* that the pacer or any member could say, or playfully shout out, to signal when the team gets distracted. Another simple approach is for the pacer just to remind the team how much time they have remaining for their meeting.

Materials Clerk

The materials clerk is the team member who is responsible for bringing the materials needed for the team discussion. These materials might be examples of student work the team will collaboratively grade, common formative assessment data the team will reflect upon, copies of an article for the team to read, other items for team discussion, highlighters, markers, chart paper, and so on.

Other Roles

Every team is unique. As teams identify their members' roles, they should consider their current and future needs and the strengths of the team members. Some teams decide to rotate the responsibilities of the facilitator, note taker, meeting pacer, and materials clerk. Rotations develop members' professional skills and build the capacity for any team member to fill in for any other member in case of absence. Regardless of the roles identified, take time as a team and clarify the responsibilities for that role. Without doubt, some of these roles are more difficult than others, and teams that rotate roles share the load with one another while building shared knowledge as a team.

In smaller schools there may be too few members on a team to fill all these roles, and in that case, teachers may need to double or triple up with role responsibilities. Only in extraordinary circumstances should team members not be expected to maintain a role on a collaborative team. Figure 3.5 can help with record keeping of the team's agreed-on role descriptions and rotation dates if the team chooses to rotate roles.

Team Name:	Role Description	Rotation Date	Team Member Responsible
Team Leader			
Facilitator			
Note Taker			
Meeting Pacer			
Materials Clerk			
Other			

Figure 3.5: Team member roles.

*Visit **go.SolutionTree.com/PLCbooks** for a free reproducible version of this figure.*

Vital Action Steps for CTE Teams

Completing the following action items will help you put the ideas from this chapter into practice in your school.

- Develop or adopt a team agenda format that will keep your team focused on your collaborative goals.

- Create, date, and revisit the team norms at each meeting at least until they become a routine part of the team dynamics.
- Develop a system to hold each other accountable to team norms.
- Develop a team meeting schedule.
- Commit to focusing your team time on student learning over teaching.
- Clarify the roles of team members during team meetings.
- Develop a roles rotation schedule that includes all members of the CTE team.

CHAPTER 4

Identifying Essential Learnings and Developing CTE Curricula

For any CTE department or team, after identifying and coalescing around a purpose and establishing processes to facilitate conversations around teaching and learning, the next and perhaps most significant task is to identify what students need to know and be able to do (addressing the first of the four critical questions). This process will look similar to the process the core academic subjects experience, though it is perhaps more challenging and a complex part of becoming a high-functioning collaborative CTE team. Although there are defined industry standards and certifications, as well as expectations in some states and countries for employability skills, there is no explicit comprehensive CTE curriculum currently in existence for primary and secondary teachers. Much time and commitment will be necessary to define what students are expected to learn—the foundational work to building a strong and guaranteed CTE curriculum. If your CTE team has absolute clarity on what it is you want your students to know and be able to do, you will be equipped to tackle the remaining three critical questions. This chapter will provide the building blocks needed to identify the essential learnings for your CTE team.

As teachers of CTE, we know our curricula are very complex. We provide industry-standard content to learners who have varying levels of experience and background knowledge within a laboratory setting. It is up to us to refine the curriculum assigned to our program of study and modify it as necessary to meet the diverse learning needs and interests of complex student populations. This process requires identifying and aligning essential skills of each unit of instruction that every student is expected to learn to prepare them to be successful in college, career, and life.

Developing and refining a curriculum that meets the diverse learning needs and interests of students in CTE is no easy task. This work in many schools is often the sole responsibility of the CTE teacher, usually with little guidance or resources. Most schools rely on their CTE teachers to be experts of the curriculum and trust them to make the best curricular decisions for students. Fortunately, there are team options for singleton CTE teachers to gain support for curricular development, instructional practices, and student learning data reflection. Regardless of the teaming option you choose, the first step should always be identifying common denominators within that team. In addition, your team should establish a system for frequent sharing and feedback on subject-specific content.

Although CTE teams and individual CTE teachers are comfortable making decisions about their own curriculum, having a process for doing so will help develop consistency as team members refine their curriculum. The process must focus on establishing an engaging curriculum that aligns the knowledge and skills students need to be successful in college and careers. Without a specific process, the team will have too many variables as they attempt to prioritize and organize exactly what the students must learn.

CTE teachers and teams should follow these three steps to help develop and refine a CTE curriculum that will be learned versus what will be taught.

1. Identify the essential learnings.
2. Unwrap essential learnings to identify course-specific learning targets.
3. Develop scaled learning targets and success criteria.

The following sections address each of these steps in turn.

Identify the Essential Learnings

As in core subjects like mathematics, science, and English, the curriculum of a given CTE course is often too extensive to possibly cover in the time available, let alone to claim that everything is essential. As stated by Buffum and his colleagues (2018), "There are some standards we teach each year that are nice to know—that is, if a student does not master it this year, it will not cripple his or her chances for future success. But we know some standards are absolutely have-to-know learning outcomes" (p. 82). Many of these standards are already defined by industry certification standards or license requirements. It would be unreasonable, inappropriate, and self-defeating to expect all CTE students to learn all the CTE curriculum each year. If you have at least one year of experience in teaching, you already know you need to prioritize which aspects of the curriculum are *need to know* and which are *nice to know*.

Essential learnings are the content that teachers identify as what they expect all students to learn. Since the 2010 adoption of the Common Core State Standards, the concept of a curriculum being aligned to an identified set of standards has become common practice in schools throughout the United States. Other countries and territories also impose college and career readiness expectations to fulfill their needs in postsecondary education and the workforce. As the Common Core State Standards Initiative (n.d.) website makes clear, "The standards were created to ensure that all students graduate from high school with the skills and knowledge necessary to succeed in college, career, and life, regardless of where they live." The Common Career Technical Core (CCTC) also supports the development of commonality among CTE outcomes:

> The [CCTC] initiative is an effort led by the states to ensure rigorous, high-quality Career and Technical Education (CTE) programs through a set of common CTE standards that will better support students in preparing for high skill, high wage, or high demand careers in the competitive global labor market of the 21st century. (Office of the State Superintendent of Education, n.d.)

Whether you are provided with a specific curriculum or not, resources like these can be very useful as you start the process of identifying essential learnings for your team's courses.

When the essential skills align with Common Core or other state standards, employability skills, specific career skills, or life skills, we should help students make those connections. This sets the stage for more meaningful learning; students know they must learn the skill because it is relevant to their lives rather than simply something they should know because it is part of the curriculum and being in the class. Students must be able to find meaning in and make connections to the required learning beyond the classroom walls. In the following sections, we address four topics to consider as you identify essential learnings: career-specific standards, broad transferable skills, connections between CTE and core academics, and a protocol to identify essential learning for CTE curricula.

Students know they must learn the skill because it is relevant to their lives rather than simply something they should know because it is part of the curriculum.

Career-Specific Standards

Although there are no Common Core State Standards for CTE, there are career-specific standards that CTE courses will address. This content often makes up the bulk of CTE curricula and directly prepares students for work or continued education in a chosen field. The alignment of career-specific content with the expectations or requirements of that career is essential, especially when a program coordinates with a college, university, or professional organization for students to earn dual credit or technical certifications. For example, high school welding programs need to align their standards with the American Welding Society certification standards (available at www.aws.org) to properly prepare students to become certified welders. A pathway to a career in hospitality and tourism would align standards with the American Hotel and Lodging Educational Institute for certification (available at www.ahlei.org). An emergency medical technician (EMT) program would align with the National Registry of Emergency Medical Technicians (available at www.nremt.org/rwd/public). Many CTE programs coordinate with organizations that guide students who work during their high school years to help them obtain credentials by the time they graduate.

Broad Transferable Skills

As previously stated, identifying the common denominators within a CTE team does not have to be a difficult task if the focus is less on content-specific skills and more on broad transferable skills that students need to possess to be successful in college and career. These types of skills tend to be universal among different programs of study. Possible broad transferable skills that CTE teams might identify include employability and 21st century skills such as critical thinking, communication, and technology skills, as well as social-emotional skills. Anthony Carnevale, Tamara Jayasundera, and Andrew Hanson (2012) discuss how CTE should be enhanced by partnerships to help with employability skills. In addition, they say:

> The National Association of Colleges and Employers (NACE) found that the two most important skills employers were looking for were "Ability to work in a team structure" and "Ability to verbally communicate with persons inside and outside the organization." It would be a mistake, therefore, to assume that institutions—at any skill level—should focus only on developing occupational skills. (p. 38)

In 2012, 15 percent of fifteen- to twenty-nine-year-old citizens in the United States were neither employed nor in school, and 48 percent of high school dropouts in the

United States earned less than half the national median (Organisation for Economic Co-operation and Development, 2014). Further:

> The United States is currently at its lowest point of youth participation in the workplace that our country has ever seen. The summer job, that was once a rite of passage for most teenagers, is now an exception and not the rule. Only about 1/3 of today's students experience the world of work while in high school. And that number is less for our students of color and those at or below the poverty line. (Stump, 2019)

The research is clear: CTE teachers have the opportunity and expertise to prepare students with important employability skills that enable them to be successful in their chosen careers, start their careers during high school, and avoid being part of the preceding statistics. Studies reviewed by the U.S. Department of Education found that "eight years after their expected graduation date, students who focused on career and technical education (CTE) courses while in high school had higher median annual earnings than students who did not focus on CTE" (U.S. Department of Education, 2019).

When identifying skills students need to learn, use the following two questions to guide collaborative decisions.

1. What are the essential learnings our courses have in common?
2. What essential skills do students learn in one course that might be valuable to teach in another course?

The Perkins Collaborative Resource Network developed an employability skills framework to describe three categories of nine employability skills that students should possess to be college and career ready. Table 4.1 (page 64) displays the nine skills with their descriptions. This table provides ideas and a starting point for CTE teams to identify common essential skills students are expected to learn in their courses.

To assist you in identifying broad transferable skills, here are some resources your team might find useful.

- Perkins Collaborative Resource Network (https://cte.ed.gov)
- P21 Partnership for 21st Century Learning (www.battelleforkids.org /networks/p21)
- Collaborative for Academic, Social, and Emotional Learning (CASEL; www.casel.org)
- Common Core State Standards Initiative (www.corestandards.org)

Table 4.1: Employability Skills Framework

Category	Employability Skills	Indicators of Learning
Effective Relationships	Personal Qualities	• Demonstrates responsibility and self-discipline • Adapts and shows flexibility • Works independently • Demonstrates a willingness to learn • Demonstrates integrity • Demonstrates professionalism • Takes initiative • Displays positive attitudes and sense of self-worth • Takes responsibility for professional growth
	Interpersonal Skills	• Understands teamwork and works with others • Responds to customer needs • Exercises leadership • Negotiates to resolve conflicts • Respects individual differences
Applied Knowledge	Applied Academic Skills	• Uses reading skills • Uses writing skills • Uses mathematical strategies and procedures • Uses scientific principles and procedures
	Critical Thinking Skills	• Thinks critically • Thinks creatively • Makes sound decisions • Solves problems • Reasons • Plans and organizes
Workplace Skills	Resource Management	• Manages time • Manages money • Manages materials • Manages personnel
	Information Use	• Locates information • Organizes information • Uses information • Analyzes information • Communicates information
	Communication Skills	• Communicates verbally • Listens actively • Comprehends written material • Conveys information in writing • Observes carefully
	Systems Thinking	• Understands and uses systems • Monitors systems • Improves systems
	Technology Use	• Understands and uses technology

Source: Perkins Collaborative Resource Network, n.d.a.

Connections Between CTE and Core Academics

Schoolwide, teachers review their curriculum to identify essential learnings. Part of this process is to find skills that give students leverage in other courses, in college, and, often, in life. By working collaboratively with each other and with core academic peers, CTE teachers in our schools find that there are abundant skills in CTE courses that overlap with the core academics and provide that leverage that prepares students for college and careers. For example, non-fiction writing is a broadly applicable skill that is of great benefit to students. Examples of non-fiction writing in CTE include written explanations, presentations on budgets, written proposals, insurance claims, estimates, letters of application, and résumés. Based on a study by Douglas Reeves (2004), "Reviews of accountability data from hundreds of schools reveal the schools with the greatest gains in achievement consistently employ common assessments, non-fiction writing, and collaborative scoring by faculty" (DuFour et al., 2016, p. 144). Non-fiction writing is a natural fit in CTE courses. Everything read and learned in a CTE course is focused on non-fiction passages. Once students are reading non-fiction materials, the next step is to have them create their own examples of similar content with something relating to the assignment or to life. DuFour and colleagues (2016) offer a set of questions interdisciplinary teams can entertain; these questions are equally appropriate for a CTE team to ask: "How will we know if our students are becoming better writers? What criteria will we use to assess the quality of student writing?" (pp. 62–63).

Following are some examples of core academic subjects and the essential skills that are connected to them in CTE content.

- **Mathematics:** labor rates, insurance rates, interest rates, income and expenses, cost of supplies and equipment, personal or small business budgets, invoices, estimates, imperial and metric measurements, volume, ratios, and so on

- **Non-fiction writing:** letters of interest or application for jobs, résumés, citations and references, estimates, advertisements for job openings, advertisements to sell products or services, directions to complete a task, job descriptions, skill requirements, and so on

- **Reading:** research, technical bulletins, blogs, directions, safety manuals, case studies, and so on

- **Science:** experimenting, asking and defining problems, analyzing and interpreting data, developing and using models

- **Social studies:** research, economics, graphing, summarizing, predicting, analyzing, formulating, and so on

Although most CTE courses apply mathematics, literacy, and science concepts within assignments and projects, most CTE teachers tend to not explicitly address the Common Core or other state, provincial, or nationwide academic standards within their curriculum and instruction. There are a variety of reasons for this. Some CTE teachers feel there is not enough time to include connections to the academic curriculum. Some do not feel confident enough with the academic content to teach it. Whatever the reason, if CTE teachers truly want to prepare their students for college and careers, they need to emphasize how and why mathematics, literacy, and science skills are integrated in CTE curricula. Students need to understand how those skills, in conjunction with CTE content, will build their success in other courses and in high-stakes exams like the ACT, SAT, and professional certifications.

In some cases, states and provinces provide alignment documents explicating the connections between CTE curricula and core academic standards. For example, Virginia and Georgia both provide standards for CTE courses, as well as documentation of connections between the CTE and academic standards (Georgia Department of Education, 2019; Virginia Department of Education [VDOE] CTE Resource Center, 2019j). Virginia's agricultural science and technology programs both have standards requiring that students demonstrate measuring skills, which aligns with specific state mathematics standards.

Where the Common Core State Standards have been adopted, teachers will find that there are many areas of overlap between the standards and CTE content. Some examples appear in figure 4.1.

Mathematics Standards

- Represent and interpret data.
- Solve problems involving measurement and conversion of measurements.
- Understand concepts of angle and measure angles.
- Understand the concept of volume.
- Generate and analyze patterns.

English Language Arts Standards

- Cite specific textual evidence to support analysis of science and technical texts, attending to the precise details of explanations or descriptions.
- Determine the meaning of symbols, key terms, and other domain-specific words and phrases as they are used in a specific scientific or technical context related to texts and topics.
- Translate quantitative or technical information expressed in words in a text into visual form (for example, a table or chart) and translate information expressed visually or mathematically (such as in an equation) into words.

Source: Adapted from Common Core State Standards Initiative, n.d.

Figure 4.1: Common Core examples.

There are many methods and resources CTE teachers and teams can use to identify connections between their curricula and academic or nationally normed learning standards. To do this work properly, the teachers who teach the curriculum must gather current resources and materials and commit to using them. We acknowledge some school districts and states that have been working on making the connections with CTE and core curricula, but we also caution CTE teachers not to wait for someone else to do this work. When this work is done by the district or state, it can be a resource a team uses that complements their own work. Some districts have organized a curriculum review and include teachers of CTE in these efforts; this is a practice we also support. A district may provide a protocol for identifying essential learnings, which is a great start. However, if the teachers teaching the content on a daily basis are not involved in these processes, they will lack the clarity that is gained in the process.

A Protocol to Identify Essential Learning for CTE Curricula

Once a CTE teacher or team has determined that a skill or understanding is essential, they must guarantee all students will learn the content that supports that skill or understanding. At this point, there is no negotiating about the essential learning for a specific course, only conversations and instructional decisions about meeting the learning needs of individuals or groups of students.

> Will this skill prove to be valuable when a student takes a high-stakes test or earns a certification?

The protocol for identifying essential learning includes four *look-fors*. Larry Ainsworth (2003) references the first three—endurance, leverage, and readiness. DuFour and colleagues discuss the fourth criteria—high stakes—in *Learning by Doing* (DuFour et al., 2016). The following criteria provide information to make consistent decisions when a CTE teacher or team is empowered to determine if a skill is essential.

- **Endurance:** Will this skill prove to be valuable beyond a single test date?
- **Leverage:** Will this skill prove to be valuable in other disciplines?
- **Readiness:** Will this skill prove to be valuable for success in the next level of instruction, college, or career?
- **High Stakes:** Will this skill prove to be valuable when a student takes a high-stakes test or earns a certification?

Ideally the teacher or team should be able to answer yes to all four questions and be able to explain why they said yes to each question. This system should be used as vetting criteria to determine if a skill is essential. The questions can be used for CTE programs of study or any other curriculum represented by the team. If a team commits to using the same questions for vetting each skill, the identification process will be consistent. Figure 4.2 provides examples of a few essential CTE skills that may meet three or more of these criteria.

Programs of Study	Essential Learnings
Agricultural Science and Technology	Demonstrate measuring skills (VDOE CTE Resource Center, 2019b).
Accounting	Identify the basic financial statements. Identification should include the balance sheet, income statement, statement of stockholders' equity, statement of cash flows, and the interrelationships among them (VDOE CTE Resource Center, 2019a).
Consumer and Family Resources	"Apply time-management, organizational, and process skills to prioritize tasks and achieve goals" (National Association of State Administrators of Family and Consumer Sciences, 2018, p. 9).
Home Health Aide	Demonstrate proper hand-washing techniques (VDOE CTE Resource Center, 2019f).
Small Animal Care	Explain the considerations involved in selecting a dog (VDOE CTE Resource Center, 2019i).

Figure 4.2: Sample CTE essential skills.

As CTE teachers work through their curricula and identify the essential learnings interwoven in their standards, they will realize not all skills will meet all four criteria. When there are no high-stakes assessments or certification assessments related to the CTE program of study, we encourage you to adhere, at a minimum, to the first three criteria for the identification and selection process. Gayle Gregory, Martha Kaufeldt, and Mike Mattos (2016) state:

> When a standard fulfills all three of these criteria, educators can consider it a non-negotiable essential standard. When a standard fulfills two of the three criteria, it is more likely to be an important standard. If the standard appears to really only fulfill one of the three criteria points, it probably is a nice-to-know standard (p. 82).

It is vital that the CTE teacher or team doing this work maintain a record. Teams should use a simple method of keeping records that supports the work; it should not be just another form to fill out. It takes time to do this work and if there are no records, the work starts from scratch every year. A form like the one shown in figure 4.3 could be used to track the teacher or team's identification of essential learnings and the time frame for when that learning will occur. It provides an example of processing CTE standards and skills to determine which are essential. A blank reproducible version of this form appears in appendix B (page 153).

Programs of Study	Essential Learning	Essential Criteria				Time Frame
		E	L	R	H	
Agricultural Science and Technology	**Demonstrate measuring skills.**					Ongoing
Construction Technology	Define measuring terminology.	X	X	X		Week 2
Industrial Maintenance Technology 1	Make linear measurements accurately to one sixteenth of an inch.	X	X	X		Week 2
Plumbing 1	Compute units of measurement common in areas of construction.	X	X	X	X	Weeks 2–3
	Conduct measuring exercises to the nearest sixteenth of a unit.	X	X	X	X	Weeks 2–3
E = Endurance L = Leverage R = Readiness H = High Stakes						

Source for standards: *VDOE CTE Resource Center, 2019b, 2019d, 2019g, 2019h.*

Figure 4.3: Essential learning record keeping.

In figure 4.3, the standard is *demonstrate measuring skills* and the other skills are subskills within the standard; notice the subskills are much more precise than the standard. The first two subskills meet three of the criteria for being essential, but this team did not believe they would show up on a high-stakes or certification assessment. The team also agreed the first two subskills are prerequisites for successful learning of the last two subskills, so they will be taught first. The team determined their students will likely need to demonstrate proficiency on the last two subskills on a high-stakes test or to meet a certification requirement. Overall, the team determined all four skills meet the criteria to be essential, but as a team of multiple content areas, they identified the last two skills as their guaranteed and viable curriculum for all students represented by the team.

This is one way for a team with a multiple-course membership to create a common denominator. When a collaborative team of teachers of different programs of study is identifying essential skills, they must first agree that a skill is one of their common denominators across their own programs of study. To be considered essential learning, the first three criteria must be met, and all four criteria will only make it stronger. If not, move to the next skill to be vetted. It can be difficult and requires discipline to say, "OK, we don't agree on this essential learning—let's focus on the next skill." The nudge provided by a systematic decision-making process may be all the team needs to refocus.

After identifying the essential learnings for your team, the next step is to clarify and bring meaning to the essential learnings as they are delivered and learned in each classroom.

Unwrap Essential Learnings to Identify Course-Specific Learning Targets

Once the essential learnings are identified, the next step is to unwrap them to create course-specific learning targets. When teams have large blocks of time in the summer, they may want to do this work for the entire school year. Another option might be to simplify the essential learnings a month or two ahead as the year progresses. Or teams might simplify essential learnings by working month to month, giving themselves a chance to apply a newly learned skill while adjusting instructional practices as needed. Whichever approach your team prefers, it should be a team decision. This section will provide you the knowledge, skills, and tools to unwrap your essential learnings.

There are complex and simple methods to unwrap essential learnings. Buffum and colleagues (2018) advise teams and teachers to identify the learning type each essential skill requires. Thus, CTE teachers and teams can plan their lessons by strategically focusing their efforts on the appropriate types of learning. The four categories of learning suggested by Buffum and colleagues are as follows.

1. Knowledge
2. Reasoning
3. Performance skills
4. Product development

Identifying learning types is often done only on core academic curricula; however, doing so is equally important for CTE curricula. It clarifies the type of teaching and learning that must take place for and by the teacher and student.

When working with teams new to the process, we find using a simple yet meaningful approach will help to create a we-can-do-this attitude, interest, curiosity, and follow-through with application of the process. Use the following five-step process to unwrap essential learnings.

1. Refer to the curriculum document and identify the verbs in each essential learning. In most cases the verbs will indicate what the student is expected to do.

2. Identify elements in the essential learning that only require *knowledge*. This is the lowest-level learning target.

3. Identify any portions that explicitly state or imply that the student will need to *reason*.

4. Identify any element that will require the student to *perform* or *demonstrate* a skill.

5. Identify any portion that suggests the student must create a *product* to prove he or she is proficient with the essential learning.

The learning types are ordered from simple to complex. Each type has a prerequisite (see figure 4.4), with knowledge as the foundation. For example, if we expect students to reason, they must have knowledge of what they are reasoning about. If we expect students to perform a skill, they must have the foundational knowledge and reasoning ability for a skill performance.

Learning Target Types	Prerequisite Learning Targets
Knowledge	
Reasoning	Knowledge
Performance Skills	Reasoning
Product Development	Performance Skills

Figure 4.4: Types of learning.

The following sections present brief definitions of each learning type and sample verbs that may be found in the curriculum. Teams should use the verbs as a starting point for identifying the types of learning. Each time the team members find a verb in the curriculum that is not mentioned in the following lists, they need to decide which learning type it belongs to and add it to their own verb list.

Knowledge

Knowledge includes factual information, procedural knowledge, and conceptual understandings that provide the foundational content. In CTE, the knowledge expectations come from the curriculum students are expected to learn. Knowledge-level learning targets in CTE curricula may include facts like knowing fractions down to one sixteenth of an inch, knowing names of tools or equipment, recalling facts of an industry's history, and listing all of the steps to safely operate equipment.

The following are examples of verbs that may indicate that the essential learning type is knowledge based.

- Define
- Identify
- Describe
- Recall
- Locate
- Examine
- Match
- Name
- State
- Recognize
- List
- Label

Reasoning

Reasoning is the thinking that goes into the decisions and actions of a response. The reasoning category consists of thought processes students must utilize to solve problems and apply knowledge to new situations. It could require a student to synthesize multiple facts in order to reason. Some curricula expressly state when a student would need to reason, while other curricula may only imply the student will need to demonstrate the ability to reason. In CTE, one example of reasoning could be asking students to assess the risks of entrepreneurship and identify economic or industrial changes that increase risks. Another example would be when CTE students would need to reason if asked to compare and contrast careers as they determine required employability skills.

The following verbs may indicate the essential learning type is reasoning based.

- Compare
- Survey
- Differentiate
- Categorize
- Infer
- Distinguish
- Classify
- Analyze
- Contrast
- Discriminate
- Prioritize
- Appraise

Performance Skills

Most often in CTE, physical processes are how students will demonstrate they have achieved mastery. These processes include performing or demonstrating a skill. Examples of performance skills in CTE could be demonstrating the proper use of shop tools and equipment, presenting information to the class, or executing all steps of first aid rescue breathing.

The following sample verbs indicate the essential learning is a performance skill.

- Model
- Demonstrate
- Dramatize
- Perform

- Exhibit
- Conduct
- Speak
- Present

- Operate
- Represent
- Execute
- Produce

Product Development

Products are physical objects created by students. Depending on the way the curriculum is written, the product could be open-ended and based on the need and imagination of the student, while also meeting certain guidelines. Sometimes products must be very specific to meet a certain standard of development within parameters or tolerances. Examples of learning targets that result in products include: develop a marketing plan, build an aluminum picnic table, prepare and bake a chocolate cake, design a floral arrangement, or construct a map of the most logical place for a new landfill within a fifty-mile radius of your home.

Verbs that may indicate the essential learning type is product based include the following.

- Construct
- Build
- Develop
- Produce

- Compile
- Design
- Draw
- Make

- Fabricate
- Manufacture
- Erect
- Form

Figure 4.5 (page 74) is an example to help guide and clarify how to unwrap a standard that has essential learning components. Doing this work as a team will help to identify high-quality learning targets and bring clarity about what the learning will look like in the classrooms. A blank reproducible version appears in appendix B (page 154).

As we stated previously, the learning types become more complex from knowledge to product development. Remembering what Kim Bailey and Chris Jakicic (2017) say, this work is to collectively gain clarification and to identify the smaller elements of the required learning. When coaching teams, we find teachers frequently try to identify a performance skill or product when the curriculum indicates the learning only requires knowledge or reasoning by the student—they mistakenly assume the

Program of Study: Agricultural Science Essential Learning

Essential Learning Verbatim From the Curriculum Guide: Demonstrate measuring skills, compare the U.S. customary system and the metric system, conduct measuring exercises to the nearest sixteenth of a unit.

Essential Criteria—Does this standard meet at least three out of four criteria to be essential? Circle Yes or No.

Endurance	Leverage	Readiness	High Stakes
(Yes) or No	(Yes) or No	(Yes) or No	(Yes) or No

Endurance: Will this skill prove to be valuable beyond a single test date?

Yes, this skill will be necessary throughout the program of study and career pathway.

Leverage: Will this skill prove to be valuable in other disciplines?

Yes, in several other career clusters and in mathematics grade 8.

Readiness: Will this skill prove to be valuable for success in the next level of instruction, grade, college, or entering a career?

Yes, this will be on certification tests and is a lifelong skill.

High Stakes: Will this skill prove to be valuable when a student takes a high-stakes test or earns a certification?

Yes, this will show up in recorded competitions, be on high-stakes mathematics assessments, and be on certification tests in this career cluster.

Unwrap Essential Learnings

The process:

Highlight—Verbs

Underline—Knowledge-level components

Circle—Reasoning expectations explicit or implied

Box—Performance requirements

Star—Product development requirements

Highest level required learning target is: Performance. Notice there is no product expectation; we could agree on a more complex performance or product outcome for higher functioning students.

Standard:

Demonstrate measuring skills, compare the U.S. customary system and the metric system, conduct measuring exercises to the nearest sixteenth of a unit.

Skills Within the Standard	Learning Type			
	Knowledge	Reasoning	Performance	Product
Compare the U.S. customary system and the metric system.	X	X	X	
Conduct measuring exercises to the nearest sixteenth of a unit.	X	X	X	

Figure 4.5: Unwrapping essential learnings example.

mindset that if it is not difficult it must not be right. We are not trying to over complicate an already complex curriculum. Therefore, teachers should only require all students to learn to the level dictated by the standards. Teachers can use learning types that go beyond the standard to provide extension opportunities when students have already learned the required content.

Unwrapping the essential learnings is the process of identifying the knowledge and skills students are expected to learn. Larry Ainsworth and Donald Viegut (2006) define unwrapping as "a simple yet powerful technique of analyzing the Power Standards—and other related standards—to identify the critical concepts and skills students need to know and be able to do" (p. 12). All CTE teams should engage in the unwrapping of essential learning process. We base this strong appeal on a quote from DuFour and colleagues (2016):

> When developing a guaranteed and viable curriculum, teachers continually refine and clarify their understanding of what all students should know and be able to do as they move from prioritizing and unwrapping standards, to identifying specific learning targets, to creating *I can* statements for students. (p. 115)

If this work is done for teachers and not with the teachers, it fails to promote the type of refinement practitioners bring based on their expertise of what and how students need to learn in the classroom. Once the team has gained clarity on what the students will learn, it's time to set the students up for success.

Develop Scaled Learning Targets and Success Criteria

Once a CTE teacher or team has established essential learnings and identified the type of learning expected of students, the next step is to communicate the scaled learning targets and the success criteria in student-friendly language. Connie Moss and Susan Brookhart (2012) describe student learning targets as "student-friendly descriptions—via words, pictures, actions, or some combination of the three—of what you intend students to learn or accomplish in a given lesson" (p. 9). Examples of student-friendly CTE learning targets are provided in figure 4.6 (page 76). Notice all the student-friendly learning targets begin with the phrase *I can*. Beginning each statement with the words *I can* clearly communicates to students what is expected of them while also sharing the ownership of that learning with students.

CTE Learning Target Examples	
Agricultural Science and Technology	I can measure accurately to within one sixteenth of an inch (VDOE CTE Resource Center, 2019b).
Accounting	I can identify specific elements of a basic financial statement (VDOE CTE Resource Center, 2019a).
Family and Consumer Sciences Exploratory I	I can set priorities to achieve a goal (VDOE CTE Resource Center, 2019e).
Home Health Aide	I can demonstrate proper hand-washing techniques (VDOE CTE Resource Center, 2019f).
Small Animal Care I	I can explain the considerations involved in selecting a dog (VDOE CTE Resource Center, 2019i).

Figure 4.6: CTE learning target examples.

Success criteria are the indicators used to communicate to students what they need to learn and do to display mastery of the learning target. Use the following four-step process when developing scaled learning targets with success criteria for CTE curricula.

1. Unwrap the essential learning to identify the type of learning you want the students to learn (knowledge, reasoning, performance, product).

2. Identify the proficiency level of the intended learning target. This proficiency level should be written as an *I can* statement using positive student-friendly language to communicate what students are expected to master. Figure 4.7 provides an example from a print media course. There are four levels within a scaled learning target. Level 3 is mastery— the learning target we expect students to achieve.

3. Scale the learning target around proficiency. Levels 1, 2, and 4 should be scaled around the proficiency described at level 3. In figure 4.7, level 1 is *still developing mastery*. Level 2 is *approaching mastery*. Level 4 is *exceeding mastery*. When scaling a learning target, CTE teachers and teams need to reach explicit agreement for each level; list the success criteria students are expected to learn and be able to do to successfully achieve the learning target.

4. Focus on growth. Bryan Goodwin and Elizabeth Ross Hubbell (2013) suggest that, to focus on growth, teachers and teams use a level that corresponds to, "Not enough evidence at this point to assess understanding" (p. 34). To avoid the negative connotations of a 0, we recommend excluding 0 from your scale, and instead identifying another symbol or place holder to notify students of missing work.

An example of a scaled learning target with success criteria is provided in figure 4.7.

Career Pathway: Arts, Audio/Video Technology, & Communication	
Courses: Print Media, Desktop Publishing	
Essential Learning: Page Layout	
Learning Target: I can use page layout techniques to produce graphic design documents.	

Exceeding Mastery	Mastery	Approaching Mastery	Still Developing Mastery
I can use advanced page layout techniques to produce high-quality graphic design documents.	I can use all page layout techniques to produce graphic design documents.	I can use some page layout techniques to produce graphic design documents.	I can attempt to use page layout techniques to produce graphic design documents.

Success Criteria:

- I can set up pages with different widths, heights, orientations, and margins according to the project specifications.
- I can use the Type Tool and Character Panel to add and format the text in my documents.
- I can place, size, crop, arrange, and text wrap images in my documents.
- I can use only high-resolution images in my documents.
- I can use the drawing tools to add emphasis to my documents.
- I can appropriately edit the fill, stroke, and opacity of paths, shapes, and text in my documents.
- I can use accurate alignment of anchor points, paths, and shapes and demonstrate evidence of the use of the Align Panel and Guides & Grids.
- I can export my InDesign documents as PDFs.

Reflection on Learning:

Teacher Feedback:

Source: © 2020 Adlai E. Stevenson High School. Used with permission.

Figure 4.7: Scaled learning target example.

In figure 4.7 (page 77), the team has completed six steps to refine their curriculum.

1. Using the essential criteria of endurance, leverage, readiness, and high stakes, the team confirmed page layout is an essential skill.

2. The team reached consensus that page layout aligns with all programs of study the team represents.

3. The unwrapping process helped the teachers build a shared understanding of what students will be required to know and do.

4. The required learning targets were identified by the team as they worked through the unwrapping process.

5. Scaled learning targets were collaboratively created.

6. Student-friendly language was used to communicate the learning targets to the students.

As you begin to refine your own curriculum, you can use the same process to identify essential learning in your program of study, regardless of the discipline, and do so collaboratively such that the team can gain clarity through the systematic process of identifying what is most essential for students to learn.

As you progress through this chapter, you may find yourself reflecting in one of two ways:

1. We have been collaborating on work like this already—now what?

2. My goodness, this is a lot of work—where do we begin?

If your team is represented by the first question, be sure to check for fidelity with the processes. If there are sub-teams, or perhaps an outlier such as a part-time staff member who cannot collaborate with the team in person, how are you including them in the processes? Other questions to ask might be, Does everyone know what the other members are doing in their classrooms to ensure students are learning the essential content? What do their student-friendly statements look like?

We have learned we do not need to attend a team meeting to see if the team is focused on their essential learnings, student-friendly statements, instructional practices, and so on. Rather, it is more effective to ask to see artifacts, evidence, or products of the team's work. We offer this same strategy for your team to consider. All team members should be able to bring their own artifacts and discuss them with their team. The intent is not to pass judgment on each other's work; instead, this can be a great opportunity for others to learn new ideas and see different practices. For example, a team might have agreed the essential skills would be the same but the way to get students to learn them could vary significantly. That's okay. Remember: the first big idea is a focus on learning, not a focus on everyone teaching the same way on the same day.

> **Remember: the first big idea is a focus on learning, not a focus on everyone teaching the same way on the same day.**

If you are the reader wondering where to begin, start with a narrow focus and start where the chapter started. First, see if your team can agree on the process to identify essential learnings and then try it out. It is critical all team members reach an agreement that each identified skill is relevant to their curriculum. If that agreement cannot be reached, move on to the next skill for discussion. Depending on your team's dynamics, you may want to select one or two skills for the following month, then take only those skills and work through the processes of this chapter.

Regardless of your take-away from this chapter, once your team feels they have consistency regarding the following three factors, your team is ready to design their instruction and assessment plan.

1. Identifying the essential learnings
2. Unwrapping essential learnings to identify curriculum standards
3. Developing scaled learning targets with success criteria

Vital Action Steps for CTE Teams

Completing the following action items will help you put the ideas from this chapter into practice in your school.

- Align the agreed-on essential learnings to career-specific standards, broad transferable skills (such as employability skills), and the core curriculum.

- Use the four criteria to confirm a skill is essential and identify essential learnings for all CTE programs of study.

- Identify at least one essential learning outcome that all courses in your CTE team share.

- Create a method to record the team's essential learnings throughout the year to avoid doing the same work from scratch the following year.

- Unwrap each program of study's essential learnings.

- Write learning targets and success criteria that align with each essential learning.

CHAPTER 5

Designing Instruction and Assessments

There are numerous books that go into detail about designing engaging instruction and assessment practices that provide feedback to students and teachers about learning. Robert J. Marzano, Jennifer S. Norford, and Mike Ruyle (2019) introduce their book *The New Art and Science of Classroom Assessment* by stating, "[This book] is also about increasing the rigor and utility of classroom assessment to a point where educators view them as a vital part of a system of assessment that they can use to judge the status and growth of individual students" (p. 1). CTE programs benefit from solid instructional and assessment practices, just like any other course or program in a school. This chapter will provide an overview highlighting best practices to consider as you work to refine instruction and assessment plans as a collaborative CTE team.

All CTE students must demonstrate learning success with content at grade level and above. These successes are often measured by a student's performance on high-stakes assessments. The path to a high school diploma and beyond requires a student to demonstrate proficiency on multiple types of assessments. CTE teachers can reinforce test-taking skills by creating assessments with formats like those of the high-stakes assessments while also focusing on CTE essential learnings. The emphasis on creating and frequently using quality assessments is paramount to prepare students for a lifetime of successful learning. Assessments should be part of instructional practice, stimulate student interest and drive, empower students to take charge of their learning, and bring clarity to the student's performance in meeting learning expectations and goals. The data from the assessments must provide clear and concise information about student learning. These data must be aligned to specific learning targets (identified when the team unwraps the essential learnings) so the intervention and enrichment timeline can be focused on specific learning needs, skill by skill and student by student.

Because changing assessment practices is such a formidable task, we must caution readers up front to avoid shortcuts in the process. The most powerful team learning occurs in the process of the work, not in results reached by shortcuts. It will be tempting for teams to copy questions from books and websites, have one member create all the assessments, or verbally agree on a common assessment and then fail to use that assessment in the classroom. Any of these are indicators the team is doing the work as something to check off a list, not approaching the process as a continual lifestyle of being a collaborative CTE team.

> The most powerful team learning occurs in the process of the work, not in results reached by shortcuts.

In the following sections, we discuss common assessments, assessment formats, scaled learning targets, collaborative grading, and instruction that aligns with assessment.

Common Assessments

Mattos and colleagues (2016) mention three components of a common assessment:

> To gather evidence of the proficiency of students who are in the same curriculum and who are expected to acquire the same knowledge and skills, at the same time or within a very narrow window of time, by two or more instructors. (p. 92)

Common assessment within CTE curricula should assume a very similar definition with one caveat. Because CTE teams usually represent a number of different career pathways, the teachers on the team need to first identify their common essential learning common denominators so they can craft a common assessment plan.

We have worked with teams and schools where there is resistance to the practice of designing and using common assessments. In those cases, we challenge, How will the team increase student learning if they refuse to measure the curriculum they have in common? It is important to mention that collaboratively building assessments will not automatically provide the needed data teams are looking for to advance student learning. Kay Burke (2010) explains "common assessments will not be valid unless they measure what they were supposed to measure" (p. 28). By identifying the essential learning common denominators and establishing scaled learning targets with success criteria, a CTE team will know exactly what they want to measure.

Just as in other subjects, CTE students must demonstrate proficiency on standardized high-stakes assessments in multiple content areas and grade levels. CTE programs of study provide opportunities for students to earn a certification for gainful employment and in some cases college credit. Many of the certificating programs of study require students to successfully pass a written standardized assessment as part of the certification process. Thus, we recommend that CTE teams prepare students for these high-stakes exams by using similar formats and questions in their common assessments.

Many high-stakes assessment designers and states that use high-stakes assessments offer a blueprint or technical guide of their assessment profile. Studying these documents as a team can help prepare teams to write assessments and develop assessment questions that have some semblance to high-stakes test questions. In addition to released test questions from states and companies, your team could use free resources from the National Center for Education Statistics (nces.ed.gov) or an online item bank such as Problem-Attic (problem-attic.com). Both sites host thousands of sample test questions your team can study to gain an understanding of standardized question formats.

Test blueprints and technical guides vary greatly from one state to the next and among various testing companies. Some blueprints are very detailed while others take a more simplistic approach. Reporting categories (broad topics) of standards that will be tested appear on most blueprints. Details that may or may not be included are the types and format of questions, the number of questions, and the weight the questions have on the overall assessment results. Figure 5.1 (page 84) is a hypothetical example of a test blueprint for a mathematics exam. The details in this chart include the reporting category, the numbers of the standards to which the questions are aligned, the formats of the questions, the Webb's Depth of Knowledge (DOK) range for the questions, the number of questions, the number of points available, and the percentage of the test that set of questions makes up.

Other documents provide Lexile reading levels, the use of graphics at different grade levels, the format of the assessment, and how they use different vocabulary words from one grade level to the next. While test blueprint documents are often extensive (sometimes over five hundred pages), there is no need to read through them page by page. These documents are usually available in electronic formats, which users can search relatively easily. Technical guides offer incredible detail about the structure and format of assessments. Teams can use these details to mimic high-stakes assessment question formats for CTE content. All CTE teams should study and use

Reporting Category	Standards	Format of Questions	DOK Levels	Number of Questions	Points on Test	Percentage of Test
Numbers Number Sense Computation and Estimation	7.1 7.2 7.3 7.5a–c	Multiple Choice	1–2	14	14	23
Measurement	7.6 7.7a–b 7.8	Constructed Response	1–3	15	22	35
Probability	7.12 7.13	Constructed Response Multiple Choice	1–3	6	12	19
Algebra	7.14	Multiple Choice	1–2	8	8	13
Justification and Explanation	7.15	Constructed Response	1–3	3	6	10

Figure 5.1: Example of a high-stakes mathematics test blueprint.

their states' blueprint information, if it is available, in an effort to create balance in their assessment models. Although much of the content in CTE curricula requires a demonstrated performance of a skill, students should still have opportunities to show their learning with standardized question formats. A balanced assessment model involves multiple methods, including the same assessment methods students are expected to perform on high-stakes assessments. This approach not only teaches the student the CTE content but helps the student develop test-taking skills.

Do not wait until testing season starts to do a study of assessments. Waiting sends a message to the students that you are only concerned about the year-end assessments. Assessment—from high-stakes exams that measure a school's success to short classroom quizzes that may not affect students' grades—is important enough that it should be a focus area for teams and their students throughout the year. Our CTE teams use the format of high-stakes assessments on five to fifteen assessment questions at least once a month. Students build confidence through familiarity with the forms of the assessment questions, and our teachers know the students are much better prepared because they have practiced. Once the essential learnings are identified and unwrapped, it's time to develop assessment questions and eventually an assessment.

Frequently we hear teams say they are frustrated that their students can demonstrate concepts, content, and skills during class, but are unable to demonstrate their learning when answering the questions on a certification test. When this happens, teams must reflect on their teaching and assessing practices with questions such as the following.

- What knowledge or skills might we teach better?
- How might we provide students practice test situations so they will be confident taking the standardized test or certification exam?

These questions are for team discussion and to make team decisions around their practice of developing assessments. It does not mean every assessment must look like a standardized assessment. However, if students do not have opportunities to practice in class, then where will they get the needed testing practice?

See the following eleven-step plan for developing and administering assessments with a high-stakes format.

1. Gather assessment materials, blueprints, technical reports, and examples of assessment questions that are similar to those on a certification or high-stakes assessment and that are aligned to your CTE curriculum. For example, a teacher of nursing would reference the blueprints and technical assessment bulletins for nursing certification.

2. Study the material and focus on a few details at a time that the team feels they can replicate and practice with students in a short time frame (do not worry about reading the whole technical document). For example, if you teach a law enforcement course, you might target the requirements for conducting an immediate threat assessment of the officer's surroundings.

3. Practice matching the format of some team assessment questions to the format of the high-stakes assessment questions.

4. Agree on how many high-stakes format questions the team will use in a specified time frame. In one of our schools, the agreement was to have fifteen questions each month on CTE essential learnings.

5. Develop a scaled learning target that will provide clarity on different levels of student learning.

6. Test the test by administering the assessment questions to each teacher on the team before administering it to students.

7. Engage in a team discussion about the experience of taking the assessment; revise questions if appropriate.

8. Teach the content to the CTE students.

9. Administer the assessment during a specified time frame.

10. Analyze the assessment data using an agreed-on data-analysis protocol.

11. Develop a plan of action based on the data analysis.

Visit go.SolutionTree.com/PLCbooks for a free reproducible version of this process.

A CTE team's approach to developing common assessments may vary depending on the team's makeup, from singleton teachers to a team of teachers teaching the same pathway or program of study. For a team of CTE singleton teachers, the common assessments are usually more focused on common skills that are not specific to a particular course. These skills may include presenting information, reading technical material, and working collaboratively with others. A team of teachers teaching the same pathway should have the same content and skill essential learnings with similar expectations for learning outcomes. Depending on the makeup of the team, the content or skills may be focused on the use of certain tools, lifting objects, or appropriate and safe use of certain equipment. As you consider this chapter's focus and your team's role in developing assessments, consider figure 5.2, in which we rate the level of difficulty of various tasks. Some of the models and strategies are less complicated when working with a team, and some are more difficult when a team is involved. Where *not recommended alone* is placed under the number, consider mastering that strategy but move quickly to take on more challenge to stretch the team's comfort levels.

As teams develop common assessments, they should consider both formative assessments and summative assessments.

Formative Assessments

Formative assessments are part of the instructional process, not something to be completed at the end of a semester or instructional unit. Mattos and colleagues (2016) explain that "a *formative assessment* is an assessment *for* learning" (p. 92). Whether students are asked a few questions about their current understanding of a topic or required to perform a specific task to display their skill development, formative assessments are designed to check students' progress toward achieving an identified course learning target. Frequent assessments that are aligned to essential learning outcomes, timed with the pacing of the curriculum, and targeted to the content or skill students are expected to learn, provide the best results in student learning. It is vital for CTE teams to reach agreement on the purpose of team-developed common formative assessments so that individual teachers and their students are clear on the expected learning outcomes. In chapter 4 (page 77), we provided an example of a scaled learning target for page layout in a print media or desktop publishing course. Included in the learning target are eight success criteria for students to master the learning target of, "I can use all page layout techniques to produce graphic design documents." Each of these eight success criteria requires some form of an assessment to check students' growth toward mastery. These assessments could range from students answering a

Assessment strategy or model for formative and summative assessments	What are your team's roles with team assessments?				
	Singleton teacher—no team	Team of all singleton teachers	Team with singleton teachers and same-program teachers	Team of teachers teaching the same program	Team of teachers teaching a pathway of programs
Common start to finish assessment with others	3	3	2	1	2
Common format but no common questions with other teachers	3	2	2	2 N/R	2
Common assessment at least once a month	3	3	2	1	1
Some questions in common	3	2	2	1 N/R	1
Aligning with high-stakes or certification question formats	2	2	2	2	2
A portion of the assessment format in common	2	2	2	1 N/R	1
Assessments requiring students to demonstrate a skill	1	1	1	1	1
Project- and product-based learner outcomes	1	1	1	1	1

Scale: 1 = Easiest   2 = Some Effort Required   3 = Most Difficult   N/R = Not Recommended Alone, Take on More Challenge

Figure 5.2: Roles of the CTE teacher with team assessments.

Visit go.SolutionTree.com/PLCbooks for a free reproducible version of this figure.

simple two-question exit slip to producing a one-page advertisement that contains all of the page layout specifications. The purpose of formative assessments is to gather meaningful data for learning for the students, classroom teacher, and the CTE team.

With that said, teacher-developed common formative assessments that are frequently administered are often seen as the magical answer to the second critical question of a PLC—How will we know each student has learned it? To clarify the fundamental purpose of common formative assessments, Paul Black and Dylan Wiliam (1998) clarify that the purpose of formative assessments is for "assessing ongoing work to monitor and improve progress" (p. 11). They stress that formative assessments are not for after the work is done. CTE teams must keep this idea in the forefront of their formative assessment development efforts to help create a cohesive approach that is part of their instruction instead of the conclusion of their instruction.

Teacher-developed assessment results are a powerful tool when data are used for more than just grading or scoring purposes—that is, when they are used formatively. Bailey and Jakicic (2017) state, "If students think the only purpose for showing what they know . . . is to get a grade, they will not view the assessment as a potential source of useable, actionable feedback" (p. 99). In addition, the students who lack motivation and seem difficult to reach are not typically motivated by grades. There is a stronger likelihood of motivating the unmotivated student with objective and meaningful feedback and evidence they can be successful.

Creating quality common formative assessments can be challenging for a CTE team if everyone teaches different content. As we described earlier, when teams do not share the same content, their first discussions need to focus on what they do have in common. These common denominators are where they should begin to develop common formative assessments. On the other hand, a CTE team with common curricula should use their curricular guides as a basis of their discussion to identify common essential learning outcomes and what they should assess.

An additional task for CTE teams is to agree on the frequency of their common formative assessments and how many questions or tasks should appear on the assessments. We are often asked how many questions should actually be on an assessment. Our response is, How many questions will it take to convince you a student mastered the learning target? Depending on the learning target and the question format, this answer could have several different responses; there is no magic number. In terms of frequency, it is important for a team to employ a common assessment at least once a month to ensure accuracy and consistency. Smaller, more focused assessments are better than larger assessments because they are easier to manage for individual teachers, provide frequent feedback on learning to teachers and students, and provide for a richer conversation within the CTE teams. Another point to consider regarding the frequency and number of questions is the ease of administering and scoring the assessment. If it is too time consuming, some team members may resist the culture of frequent team-developed assessments.

At first glance, it can feel overwhelming to add formative assessment data to your practice. However, teacher-created assessments provide vital data to monitor student learning. Common formative data provide essential information for the classroom teacher and the student.

Summative Assessments

In contrast to formative assessments, summative assessments are "an assessment *of* learning" not *for* learning (Mattos et al., 2016, p. 93). Summative assessments are often called *exams, midterms, finals, certification assessments, state assessments, high-stakes assessments*, and so on. Summative assessments are used to assign a score or grade to the student, but little to no help is provided if the student did not perform well on the assessment.

Educators are often uncertain about the difference between formative and summative assessments. We have worked with schools where the teams create a stack of formative and summative assessments. However, no one could provide clarity on meaningful differences between the two. This is an example of compliance rather than commitment—checking the assessment box without truly understanding the topic. What really differentiates formative and summative assessments is how the data from the two types of assessments are used. Formative data are used to develop a plan of action and guide students to reach a higher level of performance. Summative data are used to assign grades, points, or scores before the teacher and students move forward in the curriculum.

> **What really differentiates formative and summative assessments is how the data from the two types of assessments will be used.**

In CTE, it may be challenging to have team-developed common summative assessments if there is only one teacher for each program of study. However, teams could agree on a common format for their summative assessments. Your team should discuss what elements of a common summative assessment might be appropriate for your team. For example, a CTE team comprised of all singleton teachers might agree that they will all assess student learning using a similar style of a four-point scaled learning target. If common summative assessments are not currently an option for your team, then your team might consider agreeing on a portion of the summative assessments having a common format or sharing common questions. For example, your team could agree that you will assess your common denominators using the same format and questions for the first half of the assessment, but will remain course-specific for the remainder of the assessment. Agreeing on the format allows teams of teachers who teach different programs of study to work collaboratively using the best practices for teaching, learning, and assessing.

Assessment Formats

To best assess student learning, collaborative teams must create assessments that replicate the format of high-stakes assessments with some level of frequency (see page 82). Matching the format of high-stakes assessments at least a few times throughout a course will help to develop a routine practice for the CTE team. These assessment formats are also somewhat easy to score as a team, especially when they use a limited number of questions on a limited number of learning targets. Our teams who agreed to assess up to five essential learning targets with up to fifteen questions once a month found the data they collected provided meaningful feedback to reflect on their professional practice of ensuring students learn at high levels. In addition, students used those data to develop their own learning improvement plans. Although these assessments worked well to increase student performance, the teams also used other assessment formats more frequently—the shorter the assessment timeline, the quicker the feedback, and the quicker the feedback, the quicker a plan of action is developed for each student.

Much of what is taught in CTE cannot be measured by a standardized assessment. CTE programs of study are rich with student-performance criteria and often require project- and product-based learner outcomes. Therefore, it is not wise to use only one format of assessment. There must be assessments that require students to demonstrate skills and the ability to perform certain tasks while meeting specific expectations of the standard and within specified time frames.

Determining if the assessment matches the expected learning does not have to be complicated, and there are many great resources to help guide a team through this process. Two resources that we recommend are *Simplifying Common Assessment* (Bailey & Jakicic, 2017) and *The New Art and Science of Classroom Assessment* (Marzano et al., 2019). The constant question for teams is, Does the assessment model align with the learning targets? It is a true mismatch if a student is only assessed with a paper-and-pencil assessment on a skill such as painting a car, which would be considered under-assessing. The same would be true for giving a student a performance assessment on factual knowledge such as the meaning of *MPG* in the context of automobile fuel efficiency, which is an example of over-assessing. Teams need to avoid over- or under-assessing students and wasting time with assessment methods that don't match the essential learning. Use table 5.1 as a basic guide on aligning assessment types to learning targets.

Table 5.1: Matching Assessment Formats to Learning Targets

Learning Target Types	Assessment Format Examples	Examples of What the Questions Must Confirm
Knowledge	Multiple choice, selected constructed response, short answer, matching, personal responses	The student can recall information; identify specific parts, names, and functions; and know the facts.
Reasoning	Short answer, long answer, written responses, performing a mental task, personal communication	The student can analyze, compare, contrast, problem solve, reason, generate an original response, differentiate, analyze, and appraise.
Performance Skills	Questions or activities that require a student to perform something	The student can model, demonstrate, exhibit, speak, and operate.
Product Development	Extended written responses; performance assessment requiring the development of a project or product	The student can create and deliver a product that meets certain criteria. These assessments may need to assess the student's ability to construct, develop, compile, design, and manufacture.

Assessing Student Learning Using Scaled Learning Targets

An important step in the CTE instruction and assessment process is assessing and providing feedback to students on their growth toward mastering expected course learning targets. It is our experience that CTE teachers are familiar with rubrics and use them with varying levels of confidence and success to score student projects, products, and processes with the ultimate purpose to evaluate learning. A scaled learning target (see chapter 4, page 75) works in a similar way as a rubric; however, as Wendy Custable (2019) describes in *Proficiency-Based Grading in the Content Areas*, "instead of using a rubric for each assignment, project, or presentation, there are scaled proficiency and success criteria for each assessed learning target" (p. 45). Scaled learning targets are designed to assess proficiency and provide feedback to students on where they are in their learning. If students have not yet mastered the learning target, it should communicate the success criteria they need to address to grow toward mastery.

A scaled learning target with success criteria is not a checklist or a points-collection tool that assesses one specific assignment or project. For a scaled learning target to successfully assess and provide feedback to students on their progress toward mastering the essential skills of the program of study, it must include the criteria students must complete to successfully master them. Because scaled learning targets are designed to clearly communicate where students are in their learning compared to where they need to be, they are able to continually check their growth toward ultimately achieving the essential skills of the program of study. Custable (2019) lists three elements that a scaled learning target should include to aid in clearly communicating to students what they need to know and be able to do to master the intended learning.

1. The learning target is phrased positively ("I can"). It focuses on learning rather than deficiency and sets the tone that all students will be able to reach the target.

2. The verb stays the same across all levels, making it easy to delineate between levels. For example, in figure 5.3 the phrase *demonstrate safe handling* appears in all four levels of the target.

3. The proficiency levels are further explained by the success criteria. With this alignment, students know what knowledge or skills they need to achieve the learning target.

Collaborative Grading

Once your team has identified a common denominator or two and developed accompanying scaled learning targets with success criteria, you should schedule time to collaboratively grade assessments using the learning target as your guide. The process of reviewing student work together not only ensures inter-rater reliability, it provides an opportunity for teams to learn from each other regarding best practices for curriculum, instruction, and assessment.

There are multiple resources that can guide teams through this process of collaborative work. For example, Bailey and Jakicic (2017) state that not only should teams

Standard: Lab Safety and Sanitation

Learning Target: I can demonstrate safe handling of knives, tools, equipment, and both raw and prepared food in lab.

Exceeding Mastery	Mastery	Approaching Mastery	Still Developing Mastery
I can demonstrate safe handling of knives, tools, equipment, and both raw and prepared food in lab based on the **essential criteria and additional criteria for exceeding mastery** of course expectations.	I can demonstrate safe handling of knives, tools, equipment, and both raw and prepared food in lab based on the **essential criteria** of course expectations.	I can demonstrate safe handling of knives, tools, equipment, and both raw and prepared food in lab based on **some of the essential criteria** of course expectations.	I can attempt to demonstrate safe handling of knives, tools, equipment, and both raw and prepared food in lab based on the **essential criteria** of course expectations.

Essential Success Criteria for Mastery:

- ☐ I can explain how to prepare for and respond to accidents and emergencies in the kitchen.
- ☐ I use proper knife safety.
- ☐ I actively prevent fires in lab.
- ☐ I prevent cross contamination.
- ☐ I use appropriate handling of raw meat in lab and utilize the red cutting board for all raw meat.
- ☐ I ensure meat is cooked thoroughly before serving.
- ☐ I maintain a clean and organized lab while preparing food.
- ☐ I properly use tools and equipment in lab.
- ☐ I use the appropriate tool for the task.
- ☐ I ensure proper dishwashing, drying, and placement of equipment in the correct location after use.
- ☐ I sanitize counters at the end of lab.
- ☐ I wash and dry the sink at the end of lab.
- ☐ I wash my hands properly.
- ☐ I do not use my personal device while preparing food.
- ☐ I appropriately label and store my food during multiple-day labs.
- ☐ I limit distractions that interfere with utilizing my class time to complete assignments, projects, or labs (for example, peer-social distractions, usage of personal device, or completing schoolwork from another course).
- ☐ I clean up and stay organized throughout the lab instead of waiting until the end of the period to clean.

Additional Success Criteria for Exceeding Mastery:

- ☐ I ensure others are following proper safety and sanitation procedures in lab.
- ☐ I assist the teacher with class transitions to ensure that foods needing to be stored in the refrigerator or freezer are stored appropriately.
- ☐ I assist the teacher with laundry.
- ☐ I develop additional risk management procedures.

Reflection on Learning:

Teacher Feedback:

Figure 5.3: Scaled learning target—culinary arts.

have discussions about grading and scoring, but they should frequently discuss the following questions.

- Do we all use the same criteria for grades on major assignments and assessments? Should we allow students to retake summative assessments?

- How do we handle recording of information coming from formative assessments?

- How will we calculate grades if we don't factor in the formative assessments?

- Should we average scores or look at improvement? (p. 101)

Collaborative scoring does not have to be overly difficult or time consuming. Teams that have a routine of collaboratively scoring their assessments typically score them independently before the team meeting. Then, when they meet, they compare their scores. Often the team leader captures the scores from all team members before the meeting so during the meeting they can have a meaningful conversation about why and how they assigned a score. Another option is what we call *blind scoring*. Blind scoring student work means that teachers do not know which student or class the work came from until after the collaborative scoring is complete. The advantage to blind scoring is that it removes any potential bias teachers may have about students' learning. Regardless of whether a team uses a blind scoring process, collaborative grading should be a common practice for teams to ensure their system for grading and reporting is calibrated—different teachers assign the same score to the same quality of student work. A simple way to explain this is that my B should represent the same learning as your B. This is especially important when courses or individual essential learnings are taught by more than one teacher. Figure 5.4 captures the collaborative grading process.

The scoring calibration form in figure 5.5 can be used to coordinate collaborative grading exercises. Each teacher puts his or her scores in the appropriate column, or the recorder could collect each teacher's scores and record them on one form. The completed form serves to start the collaborative discussion. Even veteran teams benefit from this exercise. The more complex the scaled learning targets and the more variables in the assignment or assessment, the more generative the conversation among the team.

When a team first tries collaborative grading, team members might all record the same score only occasionally; most of the time each team member will have a

Collaborative Grading Process Example of a team of four teachers	
Step 1	All teachers teach the same essential learnings in their class within a team-agreed time frame.
Step 2	All members assess their students' work by a given date and use the same protocol for administering the team's assessment.
Step 3	All members pull samples of their students' work, including at least one sample that exceeds mastery and another with a lower performance rating or score.
Step 4	Each teacher removes the student's name from each assessment or work product.
Step 5	Collect all samples and title them Student 1, Student 2, and so on.
Step 6	Duplicate the samples so each teacher has his or her own copy of each sample to mark up.
Step 7	Each team member uses the same rubric to score each sample independently. Members do not discuss their scoring with other members until they meet as a team to collaboratively share and calibrate their grading results.

Figure 5.4: Collaborative grading process.

*Visit **go.SolutionTree.com/PLCbooks** for a free reproducible version of this figure.*

Team:		Date of Meeting:		
	Teacher 1	Teacher 2	Teacher 3	Teacher 4
Student 1				
Student 2				
Student 3				
Student 4				
Student 5				
Student 6				
Student 7				
Student 8				

Figure 5.5: Scoring calibration form.

*Visit **go.SolutionTree.com/PLCbooks** for a free reproducible version of this figure.*

different score or different reason for the score. As the team continues their collaborative grading efforts, members will develop common understandings and begin to grade more similarly. This is another process that should be driven by the team itself, not an administrator. In Reeves's (2003) research on high-performing, high-poverty schools, he finds five consistent characteristics in each of the identified schools, one of which is collaborative scoring of student work. Not only is this practice consistently found in high-performing schools, but it offers a level of equality for student scores and grades from one class to another and increases teachers' professional practice.

Instruction That Aligns With Assessment

Having common learning expectations means that CTE teams identify common denominators and then address the first critical question (What is it we want our students to know and be able to do?) with these common denominators in mind. Regardless of team structure, developing an instruction and assessment plan is a vital step to establishing and communicating the focus on learning in a CTE classroom. Well-planned lessons should provide opportunities for students to think, do, and reflect on their growth toward mastery of the essential skills of CTE programs of study. Custable (2019) describes the importance of weaving formative and summative assessments into instruction: "When teachers purposefully plan formative assessments into lessons, it engages students in the work and, at the same time, encourages deeper learning of the intended learning targets" (p. 50). Figure 5.6 presents the differences in instruction between traditional CTE classrooms and those that integrate assessment with instruction. Figure 5.7 (page 98) provides an example from an Introduction to Marketing course.

> Whether you are on a CTE team with teachers who teach the same content as you or not, sharing lessons and instructional best practices will provide professional growth opportunities that immediately and directly impact student learning.

Whether you are on a CTE team with teachers who teach the same content as you or not, sharing lessons and instructional best practices will provide professional growth opportunities that immediately and directly impact student learning. Teams should develop a plan to structure this collaborative work, beginning with clarifying what proficient student work should look like for each of the essential skills (DuFour et al., 2016). Once the team defines proficiency, and before providing instruction, they should also

Instruction in a Traditional CTE Classroom	Instruction in a Proficiency-Based Grading CTE Classroom
Step 1: Teacher identifies topics for students to learn in the course.	**Step 1:** Teacher identifies learning targets for students to learn in the course.
	Step 2: Teacher finds out what students already know about the learning targets and provides students opportunities to engage in that work.
Step 2: Teacher provides instruction about new knowledge and skills.	**Step 3:** Teacher provides instruction about new knowledge and skills as they relate to the learning targets.
Step 3: Teacher assigns a real-world project, possibly providing students a rubric or checklist.	**Step 4:** Teacher assigns a real-world project, and collaboratively the teacher and students review the rubric's scaled learning targets and success criteria for that project.
Step 4: Students do projects—sometimes independently, sometimes in a small group.	**Step 5:** Students begin project—sometimes independently, sometimes in a small group.
	Step 6: Students self-reflect or peer-assess on progress toward learning target mastery.
	Step 7: Teacher formatively assesses students' progress toward learning target mastery and provides feedback.
	Step 8: Students adjust their approach based on self-assessment and feedback from the teacher and peers.
Step 5: Teacher grades the project, referencing a rubric or checklist.	**Step 9:** Teacher provides additional instruction to individuals, small groups, or the entire group based on formative assessment information.
	Step 10: Teacher and students repeat formative assessment cycle, if needed.
	Step 11: Teacher uses scaled learning targets with success criteria to assess students' proficiency on the learning targets.
Step 6: Teacher may or may not allow reperformance to provide students another opportunity for a better grade.	**Step 12:** Teacher allows for reperformance to provide students another opportunity to show their proficiency of the learning targets.

Source: Custable, 2019, p. 51.

Figure 5.6: CTE instruction in a traditional versus a proficiency-based grading classroom.

Career Pathway: Business, Marketing, and Computer Education **Course:** Introduction to Marketing	
Step 1	**Day 1**—Teacher begins day 1 of a four-day lesson by communicating the intended learning target for the lesson: I can effectively explain why a promotion will help a business meet its objectives.
Step 2	Five minute bell-ringer activity: Students individually write down everything they know about promoting a business and then share their thoughts with their tablemates. Small groups then share their thoughts to the whole class.
Step 3	Teacher provides new instruction including terminology, processes, and examples about promoting a business.
Step 4	Teacher and students review the learning target success criteria for the assigned project that the students will begin the following day. Students take the last two minutes of the class period to reflect on their learning so far of the success criteria of the learning target.
Step 5	**Day 2**—Bell-ringer activity includes students reviewing the scaled learning target and success criteria for the project. Then, students begin work on their promotional poster for a business of their choice.
Step 6	With about ten minutes left in the class period, the teacher directs students to share their progress on the promotional poster with a shoulder partner. Each partner shares and then provides feedback based on the learning target success criteria. Students take the last few minutes of the class period to reflect on their learning and plan the revisions they will make on their poster the following day.
Step 7	**Day 3**—Students make revisions to their poster based on feedback from their shoulder partner. Then, students turn their poster in to the teacher for review. Then, using the learning target success criteria as a reference, the teacher provides written feedback to each student on his or her poster.
Step 8	Students use their personalized feedback to improve their poster and increase understanding of the learning target.
Step 9	While most of the class continues to work on their promotional posters, the teacher uses the information he learned about students' knowledge and skills of the learning target to provide a mini-lesson to a small group of students to improve their knowledge around brand awareness.
Step 10	**Day 4**—While most of the students complete their projects, the teacher works with a few students individually to gain the knowledge and skills to successfully complete the poster. All students turn in their final poster to the teacher.
Step 11	Using the learning target and success criteria, the teacher assesses, provides feedback, and assigns a grade to each project.
Step 12	The teacher coordinates a reperformance plan with any of the students who might want to show improved learning of the learning target on a second project.

Source for learning target: Adlai E. Stevenson High School, 2020.

Figure 5.7: Instruction and assessment plan for an Introduction to Marketing course.

develop assessment questions and activities to gather information and give feedback on student learning. An instructional plan should also include a timeline showing when each skill will be introduced to the students, the amount of time dedicated to teaching the skill on the first round, and when the students will respond to the test questions or activity. Figure 5.8 provides an example of an instruction and assessment plan for teaching students the employability skill of critical thinking. A blank reproducible version of this worksheet appears in appendix B.

Please also note that the instructional plan in figure 5.8 includes plans to address students who do not learn the skill (the third critical question) and provide extension for students who demonstrate proficiency (the fourth critical question). These questions will be addressed in greater detail in chapter 7 (page 123).

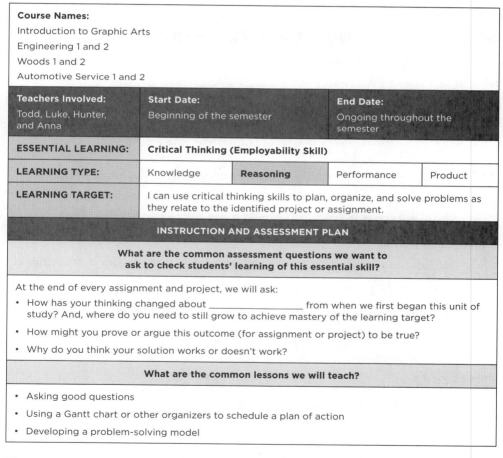

Course Names:
Introduction to Graphic Arts
Engineering 1 and 2
Woods 1 and 2
Automotive Service 1 and 2

Teachers Involved: Todd, Luke, Hunter, and Anna	**Start Date:** Beginning of the semester		**End Date:** Ongoing throughout the semester	
ESSENTIAL LEARNING:	**Critical Thinking (Employability Skill)**			
LEARNING TYPE:	Knowledge	**Reasoning**	Performance	Product
LEARNING TARGET:	I can use critical thinking skills to plan, organize, and solve problems as they relate to the identified project or assignment.			

INSTRUCTION AND ASSESSMENT PLAN

What are the common assessment questions we want to ask to check students' learning of this essential skill?

At the end of every assignment and project, we will ask:

- How has your thinking changed about _____ from when we first began this unit of study? And, where do you need to still grow to achieve mastery of the learning target?
- How might you prove or argue this outcome (for assignment or project) to be true?
- Why do you think your solution works or doesn't work?

What are the common lessons we will teach?

- Asking good questions
- Using a Gantt chart or other organizers to schedule a plan of action
- Developing a problem-solving model

Figure 5.8: Instruction and assessment planning guide. continued →

How will we respond when some students do not learn it?	How will we extend the learning for students who have demonstrated proficiency?
• Provide individualized or small-group instruction. • Provide additional opportunities for students to practice and show growth.	• Provide leadership opportunities for students to celebrate their skills during small-group projects and activities. • Provide opportunities for students to show their creative side through open-ended questions or independent projects that interest them.

What is our instructional timeline for teaching this essential skill?
At the conclusion of each assignment and project

What might we do differently next time to improve this lesson?
We will add additional content and examples to our lesson on asking good questions. Also, next time we will better weave student reflection into the lessons.

Vital Action Steps for CTE Teams

Completing the following action items will help you put the ideas from this chapter into practice in your school.

- Identify common denominators that all members of your team share and can use to design common assessments that all members can commit to administering in a given time frame.

- Research if your state's department of education or your state's testing company provides technical guides or blueprints for their assessments. If so, reflect on it as a CTE team and determine which information can provide guidance for your team's assessment development.

- Identify and design assessments that match the learning target's success criteria.

- Design rubrics around the proficiency you want students to reach.

- Practice collaborative grading and scoring to ensure inter-rater reliability.

- Weave team-developed common formative and summative assessments into instruction.

- Collaboratively design an instruction and assessment plan to teach the identified common learning targets.

CHAPTER 6

Reflecting on Data

The topic of this chapter, reflecting on data, is a foundational component supporting the third big idea of PLCs, a focus on results, and the second critical question, How will we know each student has learned it? This chapter explores developing a culture that accepts open conversations about student achievement data, uses of data, data analysis, and short- and long-term goals.

All CTE teachers and teams have or should have goals. The question is, Are the goals measurable and, if so, what are they measuring? When CTE teams and individual teachers have no system to gauge the effectiveness of their practice, they will not know if they are gaining or losing ground. Measurable goals provide an opportunity to reflect, hopefully celebrate, and raise the bar each time the goal is achieved or even partially achieved. Having measurable goals with executable action plans is vital for all high-performing CTE teachers, teams, and programs of study to grow in preparing students for college and careers. Goals identify a desired result and time frame. In this chapter, we discuss three topics to guide your team's use of student data: setting goals to improve student learning, reflecting on student learning data, and applying the results of data reflection.

Setting Goals to Improve Student Learning

All educational goals should focus on increasing student learning. A goal clarifies the desired learning for students. In other words, goals describe the near and far futures that become reality when the applied efforts are successful. A long-term goal should have short-term checkpoints for teams to assess student learning and confirm their efforts are well placed. As your CTE team collects data to monitor progress toward your goals, you will be able to adjust your efforts to meet your students' learning needs. Having goals is not about working harder. CTE teachers already work hard every day! Having clear goals helps CTE teams keep their work focused on what is most important—student learning.

Goals need to be simple, straightforward, and provide enough detail for a team to know exactly where to focus their time and efforts. However, we do caution CTE teams about including action plans within the goal. This causes confusion and often results in a bulky, confusing, unmanageable, and unmeasurable statement. The action plan needs to be separate and include steps, activities, and materials that are needed to achieve the goal. When plans and goals are combined, they can be construed as items on a to-do list. Some teams might have the false sense that once they check off the items, they have accomplished their goal and can move on to another task. If the goal is not achieved, the team must continue to refine the action steps or redirect their efforts. In some cases, the team decides on an adjusted or new goal.

For example, consider the differences between the following goal statement and the goals that include action plans.

- **Goal statement:** Student proficiency on the certification skill assessments will increase by 5 percent in the next four weeks.
- **Inclusion of action plans:**
  - The CTE team goal is to develop and administer two certification skill assessments to increase student performance by 5 percent in the next four weeks.
  - Student proficiency on certification skill assessments will increase by 5 percent in the next four weeks by increasing the amount of engaged student learning.

Including the action plan in the goal statement unnecessarily constrains the team by identifying one strategy that teachers will use. However, teams should have multiple strategies to achieve a goal because students learn in many different ways and have different needs to be successful; things that work with some students may not have the same effect on the others. Goal statements should focus on results, while action plans suggest methods.

In addition to writing goals about improving student learning within the curriculum, some CTE teams may also elect to develop goals regarding topics such as behaviors that interfere with student learning. In either case, the goals need to be strategically aligned to the overarching learning vision of the program of study. Behavior goals that CTE teams may want to focus on might be preparedness for class each day, punctuality, purposeful engagement in assigned work, self-control, and focus. If the team feels any of these or similar behaviors are preventing students from learning, they might want to develop a plan to teach and model the desired behaviors, set goals for improved behaviors, and have checkpoints or assessments to demonstrate the behaviors have improved.

Long-term and short-term goals both have a place in this journey. The long-term goal is what keeps the team focused over a longer period, typically throughout the year or semester. The short-term goals are strategically aligned to achieve the long-term goal. The long-term goal is typically aligned to school or school system goals. The example in figure 6.1 has two long-term (yearlong) goals and one short-term goal that could be repeated every four weeks. Notice how broad the school goal is and how the CTE goal narrows the focus to CTE program certifications. The CTE team then creates short-term goals to build success with the long-term goal.

Long-term school goal	The percent of career and college ready graduates will increase next year.
Long-term CTE team goal (strategically aligned to the school goal)	The number of CTE students graduating with corresponding certifications will increase by 5 percent next year.
Short-term CTE team goal (strategically aligned to the team goal)	Student proficiency on the team-developed certification skill assessments will increase by 5 percent in the next four weeks.

Figure 6.1: Long-term and short-term CTE goals.

Short- and long-term goals are effective in professional and personal settings. It may be helpful to make a comparison to personal goals to help get the point across about short-term goals supporting long-term goals. Figure 6.2 provides some examples of short-term efforts to achieve long-term goals. These examples and others can be used to explain how short-term goals must be properly aligned to achieve long-term goals or desired results. The analogies are endless. When discussing the use of goals with your team, give some thought to how you might connect with other real-life applications of goals. Using personal analogies may take some of the stress out of the conversation.

Short-term efforts to achieve goals	Long-term goal
Professional	
One goal every four weeks	One-year measurable goal
Weekly assessments	Unit assessment goal to reach a certain proficiency level

Figure 6.2: Short-term efforts for long-term goals.   continued →

Unit assessments	Mid-term assessment; goal to reach a certain proficiency level
Personal	
Lose three pounds each month	Lose thirty-six pounds in twelve months
Brush my teeth each day	Have no cavities at the next dental checkup
Save for retirement with a percentage of each paycheck	Retire with X amount of money in a retirement account

Regardless of short-term or long-term goals, or a combination of the two, when goals are achieved, it is important to celebrate the accomplishments together as a team and include students in the celebrations as appropriate. These celebrations build team capacity, comradery, mutual purpose, and accountability to one another. Working toward common goals that require interdependence and mutual account-ability is what brings a team together and builds focus. Several short-term goals combine to accomplish long-term goals. Teams without team goals have nothing to pull them together; teams achieving team goals is what makes them collaborative.

Teams without team goals have nothing to pull them together; teams achieving team goals is what makes them collaborative.

It is important for all CTE teachers and teams to have student learning goals that drive their day-to-day operations and lead to achieving semester, yearlong, and pro-grams of study goals. The more precise and targeted the goal, the more precise a plan of action can be to achieve that goal. Well-developed measurable goals require complete commitment and interdependency among the team membership. When members of a team work collaboratively toward common goals, their work reinforces the second big idea of a PLC, a collaborative culture and collective responsibility. When identifying student learning goals, program development, and so on, we highly recommend using the SMART criteria.

Team SMART Goals

Rick DuFour and colleagues (2016) say it best when identifying student learning goals: "We have found that the best way to help people throughout a school district to truly focus on results is to insist that every collaborative team establish SMART goals that align with school and district goals" (p. 89).

The acronym *S.M.A.R.T.* in SMART goal stands for strategic and specific, measurable, attainable, results oriented, and time bound. Anne Conzemius and Jan O'Neill (2014), in *The Handbook for SMART School Teams: Revitalizing Best Practices for Collaboration*, define SMART goals as "strategic goals that are part of a larger vision of success" (p. 4).

- **Strategic and specific:** The goal must be *strategically* aligned with a larger goal. The larger goal is typically a departmental goal, a schoolwide goal, or perhaps a school-system goal. Achieving the goal helps the larger organization achieve the overarching goal.

  The goal must be *specific* enough to provide clarity on what must be done to accomplish the goal. For example, *improving attendance* is not very specific. It would be better to clarify improving attendance by stating a specific number of days absent or present in the CTE class. The more specific the goal, the more likely there will be a clear plan to achieve the goal.

- **Measurable:** Most goals will have a starting point for measurement of past performance level that represents current reality. Depending on the goal, these data could come from an exit ticket, previous quiz, grades, high-stakes assessment, attendance, behavior referrals, and so on. The current reality is the latest data set available. This measurement would be noted and described in the stated goal.

  In some cases, there are no current or previous measurements, such as in the beginning of the school year or a new semester with a new group of students. Students may be experiencing exposure to the team's essential learnings for the first time. When this happens, teams need to administer a preassessment and analyze the results to determine the student's current understanding of the skill. The data would then be used for the measurement component of the SMART goal.

- **Attainable:** All CTE SMART goals must be viewed as attainable. Attainable goals are goals your team believes can be achieved within a designated time frame. If a goal is not attainable, or members of the team do not believe the goal is attainable, you run the risk of minimal effort to achieve the goal. Attainability must be defined by the team itself— administrators should not dictate goals to teacher teams, for example. When the team agrees a goal is attainable, the level of commitment increases and collective action steps can be created.

We coach our teams to write attainable goals that are realistic to their current situations *and* that stretch their thinking and learning. As a corollary, teams should never feel ashamed for not achieving their goals, especially if they see growth in student learning, and learn about their curriculum, instruction, and assessment practices in the process of working toward goals. Growth and effort should be frequently recognized to reinforce the can-do spirit.

- **Results oriented:** Goals should define a desired end result, rather than the steps the team will take to get there. The results are compared to the measurable part of the goal to determine growth and achievement. For instance, when considering improving attendance by a certain number of days, the goal focuses on the end result of better attendance, not on restrictive strategies. Thus, the resulting improved attendance can be compared to the beginning attendance rate.

> Teams should never feel ashamed for not achieving their goals, especially if they see growth in student learning.

- **Time bound:** Goals should set a timeline for completion. The timeline represents the amount of time the team will take to achieve the goal. This could be a specific date or a time frame. The timeline would also indicate if the goal is a short- or long-term goal.

Conzemius & O'Neill (2014) suggest the following questions to consider when establishing SMART goals.

- Where do we want to be?
- Where are we now?
- How will we get there?
- What are we learning?
- Where should we focus next?

Whether you are establishing a SMART goal for the first time or tweaking an existing goal, these questions serve as a simple guide for deciding on a CTE SMART goal that will have the biggest impact on student learning and CTE programs. An example of how a business education team used these questions to establish their goal is provided in figure 6.3; a blank reproducible version appears in appendix B (page 157).

Business Education: Presentation Skills	
SMART Goal Planning	
Where do we want to be?	We want our students to have better presentation skills when selling a product or service.
Where are we now?	Students stand in front of the classroom and read their presentation slides.
How will we get there?	• Identify the learning we want our students to achieve regarding presentation skills. • Design lessons that teach students presentation skills. • Provide feedback to students on their growth toward the skills using a rubric. • Provide opportunities for students to reflect on feedback and make improvements. • Provide multiple opportunities for students to present.
SMART Goal Reflecting	
What are we learning?	The data tell us that most students know how to use technology to design presentations but now they need the speaking skills to communicate their thinking to others.
Where should we focus next?	We should refine our lessons and continue to track student learning of this SMART goal for another semester.

Figure 6.3: Guiding questions for establishing CTE team SMART goals.

The following four goals are samples of academic and behavior goals to provide understanding for establishing SMART goals to meet the needs of the CTE students in your programs.

1. **Business education:** The portion of students achieving level 3 or 4 on the presentation skills rubric will increase from 25 percent to 80 percent by the end of the semester.

2. **Plumbing:** The percentage of students achieving above 80 percent on measurement skills will increase from 55 percent to 75 percent by the end of the unit.

3. **Personal finance:** The number of students able to identify four out of five components of a financial statement will increase from 148 students to 200 students by the end of October this school year.

4. **Culinary arts:** The percentage of students who demonstrate mastery of knife skills will increase from 45 percent at the beginning of the semester to 85 percent at the end.

When reviewing a goal presented as a SMART goal, it is helpful to walk through the acronym to determine if it truly qualifies to be a SMART goal. To help crystallize the importance of this close examination, imagine a CTE team setting a goal to increase the scholarship dollars offered to their students:

The percentage of CTE students being offered scholarships for amounts over $10,000 will increase from 50 percent last year to 60 percent this year.

- **Strategic and specific:** This goal is specifically about students being offered scholarships over $10,000. It is strategically aligned to an overarching goal of increasing the percentage of students being offered scholarships.

- **Measurable:** The goal is measured by the percentage of students receiving scholarships this year.

- **Attainable:** The team feels that, although this may be a stretch, they are still in agreement that increasing from 50 to 60 percent of the CTE student body is attainable.

- **Results oriented:** The team will use the percentage of students who received scholarships this year compared to last year as evidence of whether they have achieved the goal.

- **Time bound:** The team's timeline on this goal is the end of the current school year.

For additional examples, the SMART goal appraisal in figure 6.4 provides a format for the review. Appraisals are provided for each of the preceding goals. The next step is to work through the same process with a goal of your own or your team's—a worksheet to guide this process appears in appendix B (page 158). If you can't identify criteria for each letter in the acronym, you may not have a well-constructed SMART goal.

Action Plans

Once the CTE team creates and validates a SMART goal, it is time to develop an action plan to achieve the goal. In one of our schools, each team had monthly SMART goals that were aligned to either semester or yearlong goals. As the school year progressed, the team documented their efforts toward achieving the long-term goal. In most cases, achieving a SMART goal requires multiple action steps. The point person for each action step is not necessarily the person who will do all the work; instead, he or she keeps the goal alive, captures evidence the goal is being worked on and achieved, reminds the team of the timelines, communicates with the administration, and so on. Anticipated evidence could be anything from an

Goal	S	M	A	R	T
The portion of students achieving level 3 or 4 on the presentation skills rubric will increase from 25 percent to 80 percent by the end of the semester.	**Strategic:** The school goal is to increase academic performance. **Specific:** Student presentation skills	The current reality is 25 percent of the students achieve 3 or 4 on the presentation skills rubric.	Yes—This is a stretch goal for the team. The team will use these initial data to potentially establish a new goal next semester.	The desired state is to have at least 80 percent achieve a 3 or 4 on the presentation skills rubric.	By the end of the semester
The percentage of students achieving above 80 percent on measurement skills will increase from 55 percent to 75 percent by the end of the unit.	**Strategic:** The team goal is to improve this learning target. **Specific:** Student measurement skills	The current reality is only 55 percent of the students achieve above 80 percent on the assessments.	This is a realistic goal to achieve with additional instruction and interventions.	The desired state is to have at least 75 percent increase their scores to 80 percent.	By the end of the unit
The number of students who are able to identify four out of five components of a financial statement will increase from 148 students to 200 students by the end of October this school year.	**Strategic:** The course goal is to increase student learning of this content. **Specific:** Student skills in identifying financial statements	The current reality is 148 students can identify 4 out of 5 financial statement components.	Yes—It will require the team to reflect and revise formative assessments.	The desired state is to increase the number of students who can identify financial statements.	By the end of October
The percentage of students who demonstrate mastery of knife skills will increase from 45 percent at the beginning of the semester to 85 percent at the end.	**Strategic:** The program goal is to increase learning of this skill. **Specific:** Student knife skills	The current reality is only 45 percent of the students meet mastery of knife skills.	Yes—It will require each teacher to provide individual or small-group intervention.	The desired state is to increase mastery of knife skills from 45 percent to 85 percent.	By the end of the semester

Figure 6.4: SMART goal appraisal.

assessment the team developed that focused on specific CTE program certification skills, to more general student data like attendance. The column for anticipated evidence should be dependent on what the team established as their goal. We recommend creating and storing a SMART goal action planner in a digital, sharable manner so it is easily accessible for review and edits. Figure 6.5 is an example of a team action plan.

Reflecting on Student Learning Data

In their book *How to Help Your School Thrive Without Breaking the Bank* (2009), John Gabriel and Paul Farmer state, "Data are objective: not good, not bad, just facts. Data do not criticize but illuminate. Data must be provided in an understandable, accessible format" (p. 200). Data are best used when analyzed objectively. Although this is true, CTE teams—especially teams consisting of multiple singleton teachers—are often nervous about sharing student learning data. Teaching practices have long been viewed as personal and private, with some teachers fearing judgment by other members of their team—so much so that discussing, sharing, and comparing student learning data are often a stopping point for collaborative teams. However, if your team wants to develop a cycle of continuous improvement while advancing your programs of study, making decisions on gut feelings alone will not produce the long-term student learning results you want. To support your CTE teams' efforts of collaboratively collecting and analyzing student learning data, we provide two simple steps to conduct objective data conversations: (1) determine how data will and will not be used on your team, and (2) employ a data-analysis protocol to structure conversations.

Determine How Data Will and Will Not Be Used on Your Team

When your CTE team is willing to use data to measure their effectiveness, you will accelerate your capacity to improve student learning as a focused collaborative team. To use data objectively, your team should make several commitments about the uses of their data. Agreements on how your team will identify and analyze data can be reached in a variety of ways. One method your team may want to consider is to create a T-chart with one column focusing on positive or intended outcomes of using data and the other column focused on possible negative outcomes for your team analyzing their data. Once all members contribute ideas to both columns, your team should develop statements of commitment about what the data will be used for and in some cases what you should avoid when using data. Figure 6.6 (page 112) provides examples of hopes and concerns a CTE faculty may voice about using data.

Team: Construction Trades | **Team Members:** John, James, Mateo, Mia | **Date of Creation:** January 6

School Goal: Increase student performance results by 10 percent in all mathematics courses by the end of the year.

Long-Term Team SMART Goal: All Construction Trades students will increase their mathematics performance by 10 percent or more as measured on the high-stakes assessment in the spring.

Short-Term Team SMART Goals	Necessary Action Steps	Point Person	Timelines	Anticipated Evidence
All Construction Trades students will improve their math skills by 5 percent or more each month, based on the difference between their math common pre- and post-assessments.	Study high-stakes and certification assessment blueprints to determine areas to assess and format of team assessments.	Mateo All team members will learn and apply these details.	August	Copy of blueprints and plan of action for next steps
	Study the differences with Webb's Depth of Knowledge (DOK) levels and how that can apply to the team's assessment questions.	John All team members will learn and apply these details.	August	Copy of informational materials regarding DOKs
	Study methods to determine levels of proficiency when scoring assessments. Develop a proficiency guide for the team's next assessment.	Mia All team members will learn and apply these details.	September	Copy of the team's proficiency or score conversion guide for the team's October assessment
	Select a data protocol the team will use when analyzing the assessment results.	John	September	The team's data protocol
	Create common pre- and post-assessments for math each month.	James	November and one month in advance throughout the rest of the year	Copy of the assessments one month in advance each month

Source: Adapted from DuFour et al., 2016, p. 101.

Figure 6.5: SMART goal action planner.

Visit go.SolutionTree.com/PLCbooks for a blank reproducible version of this figure.

Good Uses of Data	Bad Uses of Data
• To provide feedback to CTE teachers • To help the team develop best practices • To analyze assessment questions	• To judge a CTE program or teacher • To gossip about another CTE teacher • To punish or reward CTE students

Figure 6.6: CTE T-chart for data use.

After brainstorming, the next step is for the team to write commitments surrounding data. Following are examples of team data commitments.

- We will use data to provide feedback to CTE teachers and students.
- We will use data to identify the CTE team's best practices.
- We will use our data to analyze assessment questions.
- We will not use data to judge each other.
- We will not use data for gossip.
- We will use our data to guide students to higher levels of learning and not for punishments and rewards.

The team does not need an extensive list of commitments to be effective. Five to ten is plenty to set the tone and establish a culture regarding your team's intentions for using data. Be sure to record the date of creation and the members involved so when new members join, they can be briefed on the team's commitments to data before new discussions begin.

Employ a Data-Analysis Protocol to Structure Conversations

Once your team agrees to their commitments about the use of data, you should either identify or design a data-analysis protocol that will structure the conversations around the data. Using protocols structured to provide concise feedback is critical to determine a plan of action. CTE team members will be more motivated to engage in data discussions when they see their time is well spent and they are contributing to improving student learning and the program. Data protocols can help your team objectively learn together. Depending on your CTE team's plan for using student learning data, the following protocols will prove useful. Your team can use all the protocols with the same assessment results, or as a starting point you can select a protocol that is most helpful to accomplish the team's goals.

Protocol to Find Strengths and Areas of Need in Assessment Questions

To continually improve assessments, teams should analyze the results and consider the quality of the questions and their reliability to provide valuable data. These data must provide clarity on students' levels of understanding on the standard or essential learning each question is aligned to. One aspect of this is ensuring that there are enough items for students to demonstrate their knowledge. The team needs to decide how many questions the students need to get correct to be considered proficient and if there are enough questions on the test for the team to determine proficiency. Another aspect is whether the questions ensure students respond according to their knowledge, rather than just guessing correctly. If students could easily guess the correct answer, the resulting data are not reliable. Finally, Bailey and Jakicic (2012) reinforce that the format and type of test questions play a major role in how many are needed to provide reliable information. If a question has multiple steps to solve and the students must show their work as part of the answer, the team may agree they do not need many questions of that format to confirm proficiency. By contrast, they may feel ten or more questions in a multiple-choice format are needed to determine proficiency. More complex questions can take longer to score, but typically fewer questions are needed.

Teams should also analyze the quality and clarity of individual test questions. Compiling the average score for each assessment question across the entire team can provide teams a helpful insight into its quality. These data are objective, but these data do not make the decision to keep, toss, or refine the test question. That decision can only be accomplished after data analysis and a team discussion. Before that face-to-face conversation begins, teams should capture the averages in an easy-to-use format. The protocol in figure 6.7 (page 114) is used to compile and average student results from each team member. We find these data can illuminate strengths and areas of need with assessment questions.

The team needs to agree on the ranges for each indicator—high, medium, and low. Note that the example in figure 6.7 has a twenty-point range for high, nineteen points for medium, and fifty-nine points for low. Your team may agree on different ranges. We encourage you to identify a range that best provides your team feedback on student learning and of the quality of the assessment.

The data in figure 6.7 result from a five-question assessment covering two skills. The number of the question is in the left column, the team's average score for each question appears under *average scores*, and the specific skill being assessed by each

Team: Family and Consumer Science
Content or Course: Course 8207
Date Administered: November 20

Question	Average Scores			Skill
	High 100 percent— 80 percent	**Medium** 79 percent— 60 percent	**Low** 59 percent— 0 percent	
1			25 percent	Setting personal SMART goals
2		62 percent		Setting personal SMART goals
3		77 percent		Creating a personal financial plan
4	83 percent			Creating a personal financial plan
5			54 percent	Setting personal SMART goals

Source for skills: VDOE CTE Resource Center, 2019e.

Figure 6.7: Question strengths and needs protocol.

question is noted in the last column. A reproducible worksheet appears in appendix B (page 159). Although this can be accomplished with pen or pencil, entering the data in a spreadsheet helps with efficiency when sorting and prioritizing the different columns.

The team should review data on each question and discuss questions of concern. Questions with especially high or low results could be indicators there is a problem with the question. High results may indicate the question is too easy or the question itself gives the answer to the test taker, or high results could indicate the teacher had excellent teaching methods. Low results could also mean there is a problem with the assessment question or instruction. Following a review, based on the results, the team may want to develop a plan of action to increase rigor or results. This is another opportunity to do more with assessment results than simply provide a score or grade to the student and forget about the assessment questions until next year.

Protocol to Review Question Formats

If data in the team's review of question strengths and needs (page 113) lead the team to revise or analyze certain questions, they should use the protocol for auditing assessment questions in figure 6.8. This protocol is helpful to guide preliminary discussions. The team will need to review each aspect of each question of concern individually and decide what is causing the irregular results. The team may agree there is more than one concern with the question and will then need to decide if they want to revise it or discard the question completely.

Team: Family and Consumer Science
Content or Course: Course 8207
Date Administered: November 20

Concerns About Questions				
Questions to review, revise, or delete	**Format of the question stem**	**Format of the distractors**	**Depth of complexity**	**Other concerns**
Question 1 Low average score	The stem now looks confusing to the team; it isn't written in a logical manner.	Distractors seem good.	DOK 2	There should have been better results on this question being a DOK 2 question. The team will reformat the stem and test again.
Question 4 High average score	The stem seems to be well written and clear.	The distractors were in the correct order but the correct answer was much longer than the other distractors; the team felt that gave away the correct answer.	DOK 3	Increase the length of the other distractors. The team also agreed the questions they used in class were very similar to this question.
Question 5 Low average score	The stem is good.	The distractors are good.	DOK 2	The team felt they didn't cover this well enough for the students to transfer their understanding to this question's challenge. The team decided they will reteach the concept.

Format of the question stem, sometimes referred to as the prompt, is the part of a question the student reads and responds to.

Format of the distractors refers to the incorrect answers to the question stem.

Depth of complexity refers to how complex the question is. Some schools reference Bloom's taxonomy, and many now reference Webb's Depth of Knowledge (DOK).

Figure 6.8: Protocol for auditing assessment items.

The conversations from this protocol could go well beyond the topics in figure 6.8. The intent of this protocol is for teams to have a dedicated conversation about how the questions are constructed and make adjustments as necessary. A reproducible version of this protocol appears in appendix B (page 160).

When there are flawed questions, the teacher or team should not use those data for the purpose of assessing student learning or for assigning student scores. Being transparent about flawed questions with the students will build trust with the teacher and the use of assessments. Teachers could say, "Based on the data review, it appears one of the questions has a flaw and therefore will not count toward your score."

As with all of the work of a collaborative team, it is beneficial to maintain revision records. Over time, it will be helpful to avoid repeating mistakes or unproductive practices. In addition to keeping records of question revisions, each team or teacher should keep records of the questions that worked well so they can use them again the following year. Creating a personal or team item bank of individual assessment questions aligned to specific learning outcomes makes it easy to mix and match on future assessments.

Using an alphanumeric filing system is a great way to keep and retrieve questions as needed. We recommend filing assessment questions according to the course and standard codes provided by district, state, or national curriculum guides. Using those will be helpful if and when the curriculum is changed; in some cases it is as easy as changing the folder names to keep your assessment questions aligned with the curriculum changes. For example, for a directory where you save your files, you could create a folder and file naming convention in which the first digits are the course code, the middle set of digits indicates the standard and subskills, and the last portion of the code represents individual test questions the team has created. For example, consider a business management class with the course number 6136 in the state curriculum. Within that course, there is a standard titled *effective mannerisms*, which is coded as standard 102C. The team could save assessment items using these codes; the first test question related to effective mannerisms in business management would be coded 6136-102C-001, the second question would be coded 6136-102C-002, and so on. These questions would be vetted and approved by the team as good for future use. When teachers or the team are creating assessments, they can access this directory and select relevant assessment questions. Figure 6.9 shows how this directory might look; note that this example highlights a single topic—an active directory would have many folders for different courses and for different standards within each course. The document for each essential learning would contain several assessment questions for teachers to choose from.

Applying the Results of Data Reflection

As with all activities of a collaborative team, data reflection must serve students. This section discusses three topics that will help CTE teams apply the results of data reflection and analysis to improve learning: (1) identifying questions needing more study time with students, (2) developing student support plans, and (3) informing instructional best practices.

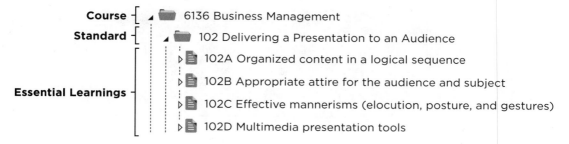

Source for the curriculum: VDOE CTE Resource Center, 2019c.

Figure 6.9: Filing system for assessment questions.

Identifying Questions Needing More Study Time With Students

If more than 20 percent of students miss a question, it could be an indication of several things. When using the protocol in figure 6.8 (page 115), teams might discover the wording or format of the question caused a problem for the students. When the review of the data suggests the questions are good, but the performance is lower than the teacher or team expects, another approach is necessary. When the questions are determined as valid and reliable, the protocol in figure 6.10 (page 118; with a reproducible version in appendix B, page 161) will provide information necessary to organize action plans. The plan may be to provide more time for only a handful of students who didn't respond correctly, or the team may need to help all students by studying similar questions until they demonstrate success on those types of questions. If the number of students needing support is low, the team will need to determine which teacher is going to help the students who missed the questions. There are times when the team will need to reteach an entire class or all students represented by the team; this would be a whole-team effort.

Developing Student Support Plans

Using data to drive supplemental support systems and resources is paramount if teams want to see increases in student learning. By analyzing data using the preceding protocols, teams can develop a plan of action explicitly targeted to students with specific learning needs. To start, data must be disaggregated "student by student" and "skill by skill" (Buffum et al., 2018, p. 107). When completed, the organizer shown in figure 6.11 (page 119) provides teams with a list of students who are still developing, mastering, and exceeding mastery of specific learning targets. The team uses these data to schedule students in different skill-building sessions and to target their intervention, practice, and extension efforts which would include helping students by

| | Issues and Questions to Review With Students | | | |
Question numbers below 80 percent correct	Vocabulary of the question	Format of the question	Evidence of covering this	Other details to address
5	This is okay; we have confirmed it is good and the students seem to understand the vocabulary.	We have double checked the format; it matches the question type and we feel the format is appropriate.	This is not good; as a team we covered the assessed skill but we are not consistent with evidence of student learning of the skill.	It was covered but not well and not consistently. We need to reteach the whole class.
7	Ten students struggled with the vocabulary.	The format is appropriately matched to the skill.	The team agreed there was consistency with how it was covered, and learning was confirmed.	Schedule the ten students for vocabulary building sessions.

Source: Adapted from Bailey & Jakicic, 2012.

Figure 6.10: Analyzing questions needing more study time.

offering more support, repetition, or rigor. This will be further discussed in chapter 7 (page 123). A reproducible version for your team to use appears in appendix B (page 162).

Informing Instructional Best Practices

While the protocol in figure 6.11 is extremely beneficial to the instructional capacity of the team, it can also be the part that causes breakdowns and resentment between team members if data are not discussed and used professionally. This is the time that is most critical to review the team commitments to the use of data and stick to the commitments. The process requires the comparison of teachers' successes on individual questions. The reason for comparing teacher results is to promote learning between one another and improve skills the team deems most essential. When teams are willing to have objective conversations and compare scores and practices, it can lead to robust conversations about activities, instructional application, frequency, use of manipulatives, and so on. When data are used constructively to improve instructional practices, it leads to no-cost, teacher-led professional development.

Teacher Name: _____

Content or Course: _____

Date Administered: _____

Question	Skill	Support Needed	Practice Needed	More Challenge Needed
		Students who score at developing mastery	Students who score at approaching mastery	Students who score at mastery or exceeding mastery

Source: Adapted from Bailey & Jakicic, 2012.

Figure 6.11: Protocol for identifying student support plans.

Since professional development takes place at the direction of the teachers, during collaboration time, it is some of the best professional development available—and it is always available when the team needs it and focused on what the team needs. In the form shown in figure 6.12 (page 120; see reproducible version in appendix B, page 163), each teacher should record their highest, middle, and lowest performing test questions. Teams could compile this information before collaboration time or do it together during the meeting. They should examine one question at a time and discuss what made the difference with the results from one teacher or class to another. When there is more than one question related to the same skill, teams should review those questions consecutively.

These data can be used for comparison purposes among two or more teachers teaching the same essential learning target. It should never be used for teacher evaluation purposes; that will only damage team members' buy-in and support for one another. This protocol only works when trust is high and teachers are willing to have crucial conversations and make important commitments about their instructional practices.

	The Discussion About Instructional Strategies That Had the Greatest Impact		
Teacher	Highest performing test questions	Middle performing test questions	Low performing test questions

Source: Adapted from Bailey & Jakicic, 2012.

Figure 6.12: Protocol for informing instructional best practices.

We have found that using data protocols has several advantages. As mentioned before, one advantage is that it can help take some of the personal emotions out of discussing how your students perform in comparison to other teachers' students. Data are also very useful for determining what strategies may have the best impact on struggling students, for learning strategies from one another, and for aligning different teachers with struggling students and offering struggling teachers support. As we mentioned previously (page 45), one of the five dysfunctions of a team is inattention to results (Lencioni, 2002). These protocols can help your team avoid this dysfunction and address the third big idea of a PLC, a focus on results. Individual teachers and teams of teachers use data to collaborate about student needs, program needs, and instructional practices, which can lead to great outcomes that help teachers as well as students grow professionally and academically. Taking a serious, analytical look at common assessment results may be an uncomfortable experience at first. As with so many things in life, practice helps to build comfort and routines for new approaches. A team that focuses on results is a team that works together in a common effort to achieve a common goal. This is a team that will be a team forever.

Vital Action Steps for CTE Teams

Completing the following action items will help you put the ideas from this chapter into practice in your school.

- Establish SMART goals focused on student learning.
- Align your team goals to the larger entity, teacher to team, team to school, and school to system.
- Share your goals with administration and the rest of the school.
- Engage your CTE team in developing a productive use of student learning data to improve the curriculum, instruction, and assessment.
- Use the protocols to engage in discussions and develop plans based on the team's common formative assessment data.
- Develop short-term goals to achieve long-term CTE goals.

CHAPTER 7

Responding to Student Learning

One of the goals of the PLC process is to guarantee high levels of learning for all students. To do so, teachers, teams, and schools need structures that guide their responses to student learning (or lack thereof). *Response to intervention* (RTI) is a multitiered system for supporting students as they learn, whether they need extra support or an extra challenge. RTI and related terms such as *prevention, intervention, extension, enrichment,* and *remediation* are important for CTE teachers to know and apply. Each of these terms fits into an intervention model. Figure 7.1 (page 124) provides a visual of where each term can be expected in a three-tiered RTI model. This chapter will provide an overview of the RTI model, the associated teacher actions, and information on how teachers, teams, and schools can implement the concepts of the RTI model.

When teachers become familiar with RTI and the terminology, they should discuss the concepts of RTI with their students. Students should not only know the terminology, but also understand that their CTE teacher will do everything possible to provide high-quality instruction and prevent them from struggling with the content. Students also need to understand the guarantee that they will receive additional support if they need it. Much of this information and the RTI vocabulary could be new to your CTE members and students. Complicating the matter further, some states no longer use the term *RTI* and now reference *multitiered systems of support* (MTSS). In general, the two models are very similar in concept and design. Both models are either an upright or inverted pyramid design. Both have more people, more resources, and 100 percent of the students in Tier 1, fewer students being served in Tier 2, and fewer students yet in Tier 3. Most educators are familiar with an upright pyramid, and now the inverted pyramid is gaining in popularity and application.

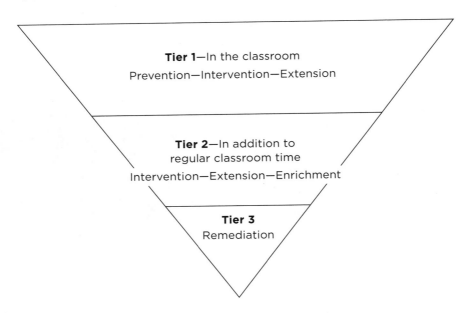

Source: Adapted from Buffum et al., 2018, p. 22.

Figure 7.1: Inverted RTI pyramid.

General Framework of Schoolwide Response to Intervention

RTI is best implemented as a schoolwide model; in this section we will give an overview of the schoolwide framework. Please note that the foundation of RTI is effective instruction. You may have turned to this chapter first with your heart set on helping struggling students, but you must first implement the vital actions from the previous chapters, otherwise your RTI will be doomed to failure. The chapters up to this point build the foundation to gain clarity on what CTE students must learn and how to assess that learning; those details are an absolute necessity for an RTI system to work effectively. The following are brief descriptions of each tier.

Tier 1

Tier 1 serves 100 percent of the student body and could also be referred to as the tier for prevention and classroom intervention. However, students needing extension or enrichment should receive it in the classroom alongside students receiving intervention. Tier 1 is the best and most efficient place for students to receive the support needed in CTE. Essential skills from the curriculum of each teacher or team are the primary focus in Tier 1. Since the team's identified essential learnings are the guaranteed viable curriculum the students will learn, all students must be guaranteed access to Tier 1 time and support.

Tier 2

Tier 2 is an increased level of support and additional resources for the students who need intervention or extension on the essential learnings. Teachers use the common assessment data to identify students for Tier 2 support and resources. The support in Tier 2 is always in addition to systems in Tier 1. Tier 2 works effectively if the number of students being served does not exceed 20 percent of the student body. Austin Buffum, Mike Mattos, and Chris Weber (2012) explain that "80 percent of students receiving a well instructed, research-based curriculum should experience success as a result of initial core instruction" (p. 61). When more than 20 percent of the students need Tier 2 intervention, it could indicate there are unresolved complications with the application and processes in Tier 1—"you don't have an intervention problem, you have a 'what we do all day long in the classroom' problem" (Buffum et al., 2012, p. 61). When this happens, one of the first things the team needs to do is shift their efforts to increasing the quality of instructional strategies in Tier 1.

In most schoolwide RTI systems, the primary Tier 2 intervention sessions will be focused on academic curricula. Still, CTE should be part of the schoolwide model by helping with study session management and teaching academic behaviors like organization, being on time, setting goals, and maintaining current calendars. In some cases, CTE teachers may cover other classes to help reduce the student to adult ratio in the intervention sessions. CTE teams should also establish their own intervention sessions for students who did not learn the essential skills in their CTE program of studies.

For extension, the school should provide opportunities during support sessions. For example, students who demonstrated mastery of essential skills like fractions may come to a CTE teacher during the Tier 2 time and use those skills to build a project that requires measuring with fractions. CTE involvement in schoolwide RTI programs is also a benefit to the CTE programs themselves because they gain exposure. CTE can boost their enrollment by exposing more students to their programs of study during support and enrichment skill-building sessions.

Tier 3

Tier 3 is for intensive remediation. For a schoolwide application of RTI, Tier 3 works best if the number of students can be kept below 10 percent of the student body; 0 percent is the ultimate quest. This tier supports students who have substantial or multiple academic needs. Tier 3 is designed to provide students with below-grade-level support and foundational skills. A sample of supports offered in Tier 3 includes, but is not limited, to "reading, writing, number sense, English language, social and academic behaviors, [and] health and home" (Buffum et al., 2018, p. 18). Tier 3 supports are always in addition to Tier 1 and 2 systems.

CTE teachers can provide Tier 3 remediation by providing employability skills, job shadowing, and career exposure opportunities. This is especially beneficial for juniors and seniors in high school as they will soon transition to postsecondary opportunities. These students' next steps are into the community, and we should challenge ourselves as a CTE team to ensure they are ready for gainful employment even if they are not on target for a diploma. Employability skills are one of the areas of CTE expertise. Parents, students, and employers count on us to make it happen.

> Employability skills are one of the areas of CTE expertise. Parents, students, and employers count on us to make it happen.

Teacher Actions

As suggested in the preceding sections, within each tier of RTI, there are various actions that teachers perform to support students. These include prevention, intervention, extension, enrichment, and remediation.

Prevention

Prevention—quality instruction on grade-level content—is the core of RTI in Tier 1. It is applied by all teachers in all classrooms, it happens every hour of every day, and it is for all students. It is important to learn about students' individual needs at the beginning of the school year. This allows teams to put systems in place to prevent students from starting another school year that might otherwise end with struggles for the student. Prevention focuses on grade-level essential learnings, and all strategies possible are applied to prevent a student from struggling in that program of study.

Intervention

Buffum and colleagues (2018) state that "an intervention is anything a school does above and beyond what all students receive to help certain students succeed academically" (p. 27). In other words, when a student struggles, the teacher responds with intervention. The quickest and most effective intervention is implemented immediately by the teacher in the classroom. When intervention is received during normal classroom hours, it is part of Tier 1. Intervention is not provided to all students because not all students struggle with the essential learning. However, there must be a guarantee that intervention will be provided to all students who are struggling with grade-level and CTE program-level essential learnings. Struggling students are typically identified by data collected from common formative assessments.

Intervention is also one of the functions of RTI in Tier 2. Tier 2 interventions are provided in addition to regular classroom time and come in multiple forms of support and resources for a struggling student. If a school has a schoolwide RTI system, the interventions for grade-level learning can be applied by the student's teacher or other teachers on the team who know the content or skills the student needs. Tier 2 intervention can also occur outside the classroom by certified professionals with the necessary skillsets to support the struggling student.

Extension

Extension must be applied when the student quickly learns the essentials or comes to class already knowing the essentials. Extension is one of the answers to critical question four of a PLC, How will we extend the learning for students who have demonstrated proficiency? Teachers must preplan for the students who learn more quickly, or they will run the risk of students getting bored and disengaging from class activities. Extension is best offered by giving students curriculum-based problems and project-based activities. When some students are receiving interventions in Tier 1 or 2, the other students should be engaged in activities that deepen or extend their learning. Buffum and colleagues (2018) clarify, "These opportunities should be based on student interest whenever possible" (p. 181).

Extension can take place during regular class time and should be applied when the common assessment data indicate that students have scored above proficiency. If your school has a schoolwide RTI system in place, extension should also be delivered during the designated Tier 2 time. When planning extensions, Buffum and colleagues (2018) recommend, "Teachers can make the actual content more rigorous; make the process or activities in which the students engage more rigorous; or make the culminating product, which applies what students have learned, more rigorous" (p. 180). As an example, a CTE team may be teaching sizes and uses of wrenches and find some students are already proficient with this essential learning. This would be a case where extension projects related to wrenches would be appropriate. Consider these extension examples.

- The CTE teacher assigns a project to build a tool board to house wrenches for an efficient checkout and inventory system. This system would provide a concise method of inventory to monitor who had the wrench or wrenches last.

- A CTE teacher assigns students to find the best replacement cost for each wrench of the same size and make as those in inventory. The students will need to research the best prices and vendors and create a form or spreadsheet with this information for the current year. The teacher could also have students prepare purchase orders to be used when needed throughout the year.

- A CTE teacher assigns students to make learning stations where the other students will cycle through to identify and learn sizes by sight and proper use.

The first two examples are CTE program specific; they help students develop skills that will be useful when they enter the workforce—organization and locating the best prices on tools and equipment. The third example benefits the advanced student and the entire class. The advanced student benefits by identifying multiple applications using nuts, bolts, and equipment to set up practice stations. The other students benefit by practicing on the training aids, and the CTE teacher benefits by having more time to monitor the learning instead of building training aids.

Enrichment

Enrichment is the second answer to critical question four of a PLC, How will we extend the learning for students who have demonstrated proficiency? Enrichment is experiences and learning opportunities the student would not receive in the classes they regularly attend. While extension goes deeper in the curriculum, enrichment goes outside the curriculum. Enrichment typically takes place during Tier 2 times while other students are receiving intervention and extension. Buffum and colleagues (2018) define enrichment as "students having access to the subjects that specials or electives teachers traditionally teach, such as music, art, drama, applied technology, and physical education" (p. 29). Notice that they indicate that applied technology and electives teachers can provide enrichment opportunities for high-performing students.

Along with extension, enrichment is critical for a successful RTI model in your school and within your CTE team. Without clarity on both of these components, you cannot respond to critical question four of a PLC. *A Handbook for High Reliability Schools*, by Robert Marzano, Phil Warrick, and Julia Simms (2014), suggests that schools should survey their community, including students, to measure the level of access high-performing students have to CTE programs of study. Schools or teams that are providing extension and enrichment opportunities well can respond positively to the statement, "Students who have demonstrated competency levels greater than those articulated in the system are afforded immediate opportunities to begin work on advanced content and career paths of interest" (p. 101).

Remediation

Students who are struggling receive intervention on current essential learnings from the CTE program of studies, while remediation is focused on skills and behaviors the student should have learned in previous years. Remediation is always provided in addition to prevention and intervention. If your school has a schoolwide RTI system in place, remediation should be the basis for Tier 3 support.

However, even without a schoolwide RTI, CTE teachers can set up remediation specifically for the CTE students the team represents. As an example, the CTE teacher may be teaching a unit on estimating that requires finding and combining the cost of parts, the number of hours for labor, labor rates, and taxes. In a high-school-level CTE program, it would be expected that students know how to locate information using a table of contents or search for this information in a software program, read and interpret the content in estimating guides, then calculate whole numbers and fractions. For example, the student may be tasked with estimating a job that will pay for 5.5 hours, at $38.75 an hour, with parts that will cost $212.00 including tax. It would be assumed a high school student could calculate these numbers and provide a customer with an estimate to complete the job. With a few related questions on a preassessment, the CTE team would be able to identify students who are not proficient in these skills. The team would then set up remediation focused on learning the prerequisite skills for specific students.

Students should be taught that when they are assigned to interventions or remediation, it is to guarantee they will learn the prerequisites needed to be proficient with the essential learnings; intervention and remediation are not punishments for learning at a different rate than other students. Students should also know when they demonstrate high levels of success their teachers will extend the curriculum to keep them engaged in the learning and challenge them to learn at the highest possible level.

Figure 7.2 (page 130) summarizes the general framework of an inverted RTI model, showing the teacher actions within the tiers.

RTI for CTE Teams

CTE teachers need to be involved with RTI as much as any other teacher in the school. If your school does not have a schoolwide RTI model, your team can and should build its own.

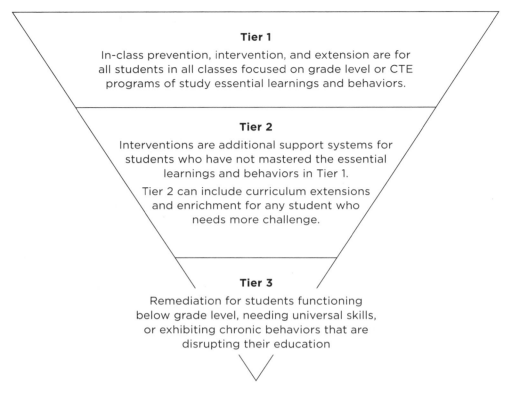

Source: Adapted from Buffum et al., 2018, p. 22.

Figure 7.2: Schoolwide inverted pyramid of teacher actions.

RTI for a team with CTE teachers should be of the same format as the schoolwide model. However, the roles of CTE teachers might vary significantly to meet the unique needs of the CTE programs of study and students.

Your CTE RTI model will be designed for and by your CTE team to serve the needs of CTE students represented by your team. The best way to build a CTE RTI model is to start with Tier 1. This tier will require more learning on your part, and more effort, strategies, foundation building, and culture building with your team. It will also require more resources than any other tier because it serves 100 percent of the students the team represents. Tier 1 is the foundation for the RTI model, and anything else built in or for the program will only be as strong as the foundation can support. CTE teams and students will benefit by starting the year with RTI in place. However, building an RTI model anytime of the year is better than not having RTI.

Tier 1 for CTE

Before building an RTI plan for your CTE programs of study, teams should develop a shared understanding of the information we have explored in the previous chapters of this book and at the very least confirm they have collaboratively reached consensus on several key ideas and the corresponding actions connected to these ideas. All the following key actions take place in a quality Tier 1 model. Unless the following are happening with fidelity, Tier 2 interventions will most likely fail.

- Develop a clear purpose for your CTE team.
- Align your CTE team goals, mission, and vision.
- Identify common denominators among your CTE team members.
- Simplify course essential learnings.
- Agree on a specific number of learning targets for course essential learnings.
- Agree on an instructional cycle timeline.
- Agree on an assessment data protocol for the CTE team.
- Design instruction and assessments aligned to learning targets and success criteria.
- Analyze common assessment data.
- Agree on in-class prevention and intervention strategies targeting essential CTE learnings.

Avoiding overloading Tier 2 with more than 20 percent of your students is best done by effective prevention and in-class interventions, which take place in the teacher's classroom where the response can be immediate. Holding a high level of consistency with the preceding tasks will help to increase the success of students in Tier 1. However, as the year progresses, a team will find a need for Tier 2 support systems for struggling students.

Tier 2 for CTE

Tier 2 students are identified by analyzing the common assessment results to determine which students need intervention or enrichment in CTE. If time is not provided by a schoolwide RTI, the team may be limited to providing Tier 2 support when they teach in common blocks of time or during planning periods when other teachers are teaching. Therefore, Tier 2 in a CTE RTI model requires all team members to work with a unified approach on essential learnings. We used measurement as an example of essential learning in chapter 4 (page 69), unwrapped the standard, and put it in student-friendly language. When that example team plans for Tier 2 support, they would compile and compare the team's common assessment results to develop a unified approach for intervention or enrichment on measurement.

A unified approach in Tier 2 means that the team refers to their common assessment data outcomes from the protocols presented in chapter 6 (page 112). CTE teams identify three groups of students: at or exceeding mastery, approaching mastery, and developing mastery. Then, they reflect on the data to identify which team members should take which roles of support. Ideally there will be at least three members so there could be one member for each group of students. In most cases, CTE students will be summoned by teachers from other courses like English and mathematics for remediation, which can reduce the number of students for CTE to support during Tier 2 time. Depending on your school's structure, you may have a small or large group of students for CTE during Tier 2 time. It is more important to have commonality of student needs during this time than it is to have a smaller group of students. In some cases, our teachers may have more than thirty students, and if needed we would plan for another adult (such as a counselor, secretary, or administrator) to join that teacher. While the CTE teacher would lead the support session, the second adult in the room would help keep students focused, prepared, and on track with the activity or what the teacher is teaching. However, your team may have more or less than three members on the team or more than three types of support needed. In these cases, the team needs to prioritize which groups will be supported first and work out the logistics of when the students will get the needed support.

If there are fewer members than roles that need to be covered, consider spreading the roles over more than one day, or have a member double up on support for two groups of students. For example, in figure 7.3, three roles for three days are covered by two teachers. There are several ways to share these roles, and the CTE team should make decisions based on their assessment data. An assessment-data analysis could show that one group is larger than the other which would need to be taken into consideration when dividing students between the two teachers. Keep in mind they should be working with the same total number of students they have any other day during that block of time. The team could increase or decrease the number of days of support in the following week. The team decides what is best for the students and what is viable for the teachers to accomplish within the given time frame. Regardless of the approach, the students should receive the needed support systems.

Working with students of mixed performance levels on the same skill can serve multiple purposes. In figure 7.3, teacher 1 has students from the support needed and more challenge needed categories on Monday, so she might support them with differentiation or pair students up as mentor and mentee. The students needing support benefit from peer instruction, and the advanced students benefit because teaching others involves articulating and synthesizing learned information, which is, itself, an act of taking the learning further. On Friday, teacher 1 has only the more

Day of Week	More Challenge Needed (Extension and Enrichment)					Practice Needed (Prevention to Avoid Intervention Later)					Support Needed (Intervention)				
	M	T	W	T	F	M	T	W	T	F	M	T	W	T	F
Teacher 1	X				X			X			X		X		
Teacher 2			X			X			X						X

Figure 7.3: Two teachers provide three levels of support.

challenge needed group and can target their needs with a different activity. You can see the other grouping combinations with this example. A similar schedule could be used when there are three or more teachers.

Regardless of the schedule, a recommended amount of support time is about thirty minutes: "Generally speaking, about thirty minutes is a sufficient length of time to provide targeted instruction" (Buffum et al., 2018, p. 187). All students should understand how their assessment results identify them for support and that they will take a new assessment at the conclusion of their support sessions. Some teams create two sets of assessment questions and use different questions at the end of a support session while other teams use the same questions to guide the study sessions. Students still need to demonstrate proficiency at the end of the support session or sessions or be scheduled for additional support. Remember Tier 2 covers the essential learnings, and learning the essentials is non-negotiable. The more targeted the support session, the more targeted the assessment can be at the end of the session.

Tier 3 for CTE

Tier 3 supports are provided to students who need them in addition to Tier 1 and 2 systems. Tier 3 is primarily focused on foundational skills and content students should have learned in previous courses or grade levels. Tier 3 may be focused on chronic behavior that is preventing the student from learning the grade-level curriculum. Tier 3 is not focused on the same things as Tiers 1 and 2. If there is no school-wide model allocating time in the day for Tier 3 support systems, the CTE team will need to be creative with how they provide their students with Tier 3 support. But first, the team will need to determine how students will be identified for Tier 3 support and identify an exit plan from Tier 3 support once the student has shown growth. For example, the team might develop a screener that assesses prerequisite skills for the CTE programs of study. The screener could be applied at the beginning or end of the school year for incoming and returning CTE students. If the screener is administered at the end of the year, the team has time to develop Tier 3 support systems over the summer and plan a team approach to accelerate some of the lowest-level learners coming to CTE the following year. The team may also consider looking for additional resources like applying for a grant to fund a summer boot camp to help students gain the prerequisite skills before the school year starts. We recommend using the same information that identifies the student for Tier 3 support to exit the student from Tier 3 support systems. As an example, if the student demonstrates a lack of understanding of a certain prerequisite skill from last year, as soon as they demonstrate they have learned that skill they would no longer receive Tier 3 support systems for that skill.

In addition to year-end screeners, the team could develop a quarterly or semester screener since student needs for Tier 3 support will surface during the school year. The use of a screener could provide needed information to the teachers who can then set up safeguards in their classrooms to provide additional assistance when necessary.

If the team elects to pull Tier 3 students from a class to provide remediation, there must be an agreement with the teacher of that class that no new essential learnings will be introduced while Tier 3 students are being supported. Buffum and colleagues (2018) state, "When students miss new critical grade-level core curriculum to receive interventions, it is akin to having students take one step forward (improvement in a remedial skill), while taking one step back (missing a new essential grade-level skill)" (p. 4).

In figure 7.3 (page 133), the schedule does not include Tier 3 supports, but there are no supports scheduled Tuesdays and Thursdays, so Tier 3 efforts could be applied on those days or swapped for any of the scheduled days. Tier 3 should be delivered with increased frequency, but if your school does not have an RTI model, you may be somewhat limited in setting up the time to support students with Tier 3 needs, and that is a very unfortunate situation for all involved. Figure 7.4 summarizes the general framework for a CTE RTI model when there is no schoolwide model in place.

Classroom Interventions

In addition to the team model, CTE teams can collaborate on responses that each teacher can use in his or her classroom. We would be hard pressed to find a teacher who doesn't help struggling students or provide extension and enrichment opportunities for high-performing students in their classes on a routine basis. However, your team should approach the development of classroom-level systems of interventions and extensions as a non-negotiable for all teachers on the team. Classroom

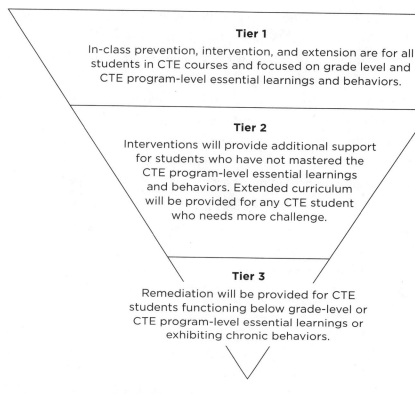

Figure 7.4: CTE RTI when there is no schoolwide model.

interventions take place within the four walls of the classroom. The strategies for each tier are different and increase with intensity from Tier 1 to Tier 3.

A network of multiple members is a powerful resource when exchanging strategies to help struggling students. The team will quickly learn they all have intervention strategies they use to different extents and will be able to learn from each other regardless of their programs of study. In many cases the entire team will adopt several strategies; in other cases a team member may find a strategy that works very well in her CTE class, and the other members wouldn't see it as a fit for them. No team members should be limited to the team's classroom intervention model, and all members should be encouraged to add more of their own strategies. This is another example of tight and loose expectations—team members must have a set of classroom interventions (tight) but each teacher can add and customize his or her strategies (loose). Figure 7.5 (page 136) provides the same design as the schoolwide or team RTI models, but the actions in Tier 1 and 2 are confined to classroom interventions, and Tier 3 is when the teacher starts reaching outside the classroom environment for intervention ideas. Using the same design as the schoolwide intervention model will build clarity and cohesion between tiers of support, for a schoolwide model and for an in-class model.

In addition, we find using this model will help focus the team's discussions about strategies specific to the different tiers, rather than a vague discussion about "what we do for struggling students." Teams must have a clear and refined practice of selecting their essential learnings and assessment practices before building their classroom interventions. This will allow the team to be more consistent with each teacher's in-class response when students struggle with essential learnings. Working on classroom prevention, intervention, and extension strategies is another common denominator for a team representing various programs of study. Any one teacher may experience a struggling student in his or her class, and all teachers participate in actively seeking strategies to support all struggling students to prevent further issues.

Figure 7.6 (page 138) shows an example of a CTE team's agreements on their classroom intervention model. The example includes specific strategies the entire team agrees are appropriate in most cases to apply when a CTE student is struggling with the essential skills.

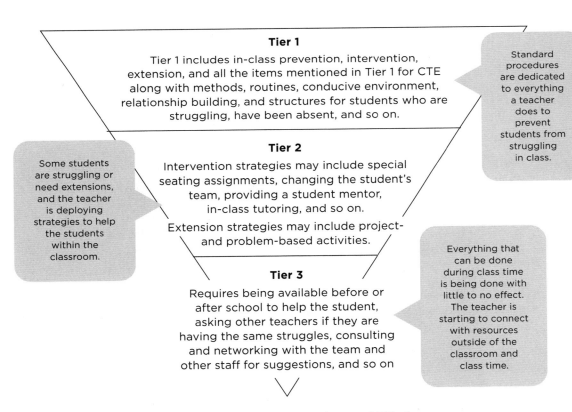

Tier 1

Tier 1 includes in-class prevention, intervention, extension, and all the items mentioned in Tier 1 for CTE along with methods, routines, conducive environment, relationship building, and structures for students who are struggling, have been absent, and so on.

Standard procedures are dedicated to everything a teacher does to prevent students from struggling in class.

Tier 2

Intervention strategies may include special seating assignments, changing the student's team, providing a student mentor, in-class tutoring, and so on.
Extension strategies may include project- and problem-based activities.

Some students are struggling or need extensions, and the teacher is deploying strategies to help the students within the classroom.

Tier 3

Requires being available before or after school to help the student, asking other teachers if they are having the same struggles, consulting and networking with the team and other staff for suggestions, and so on

Everything that can be done during class time is being done with little to no effect. The teacher is starting to connect with resources outside of the classroom and class time.

Figure 7.5: Inverted pyramid of interventions—CTE classroom.

We do not recommend using the exact strategies listed in this example because that could cause a feeling of compliance instead of commitment among the team. Instead, facilitate a discussion with your team, have all members contribute their own strategies, and build consensus on your team's model. This type of approach will more likely lead to strong ownership which increases commitment of the team membership.

> **Working on classroom prevention, intervention, and extension strategies is another common denominator for a team representing various programs of study.**

To guide the development of your team's classroom interventions, we provide the worksheet shown in figure 7.7 (page 139). Distribute a copy to each person on your team and ask them to write at least two strategies in each tier. Schedule a meeting to discuss one another's strategies and share ideas. The intention of the activity is to develop a set of in-class interventions and extensions for each tier. The team could agree on several strategies that they will all use, while maintaining autonomy for each teacher to have unique strategies the team does not want to adopt.

Vital Action Steps for CTE Teams

Completing the following action items will help you put the ideas from this chapter into practice in your school.

- If there is a schoolwide RTI model in place:
    - Consult with the administration and include them when developing CTE strategies for RTI.
    - Develop a plan to learn and teach RTI vocabulary to students.
    - Discuss with the administration the different skills your team can provide for students receiving Tier 2 and 3 supports.
    - Identify employability skills and any other support systems your team can teach to students receiving Tier 3 supports.
    - Ask to have a member of your team on the schoolwide RTI team.
- If there is no schoolwide RTI in place:
    - Develop a plan to learn and teach RTI vocabulary to CTE students.
    - Create a CTE RTI model for all students served by your team.
    - Develop a schedule of support for CTE students needing Tier 2 and 3 systems.
    - Develop classroom interventions.

Tier 1—In-Class Prevention Strategies

Explicitly communicated CTE essential skills, connecting the CTE skills to the student's life, referring to all students by their first or last name, frequent checking for understanding, seating charts, established student teams, positive parent contact, greeting students, attending student events and letting them see you are there and watching, developing a relationship with students beyond the curriculum, posting a calendar of all assignments and activities, having students keep a calendar of upcoming events, assigning homework partners, differentiated instruction, developing a systematic plan for students who miss instruction, reading students' cumulative records, studying students' IEPs and 504 Plans

Tier 2—In-Class Intervention Strategies

Additional support on essential skills for specific students, changing the seating chart or team assignments, one-on-one conversations about why the student is struggling, assigning peer tutors or mentors, providing additional manipulatives, proximity to the student, more frequent checks for understanding, student signals for when he or she is not understanding, helping the student develop a learning plan, referring to the CTE team's classroom intervention model for more ideas

Tier 3—Reaching Outside the Class for Advice

(Contact with others is to gain understanding and share information, not for others to fix the concerns.)

Meeting with the CTE team to gain new ideas for in-class interventions, contacting special education for new ideas on interventions and supports, contacting parents to let them know their child is struggling and ask for input, checking with the student's other teachers, contacting the school counselor, contacting the appropriate administrator

Figure 7.6: CTE in-class intervention example.

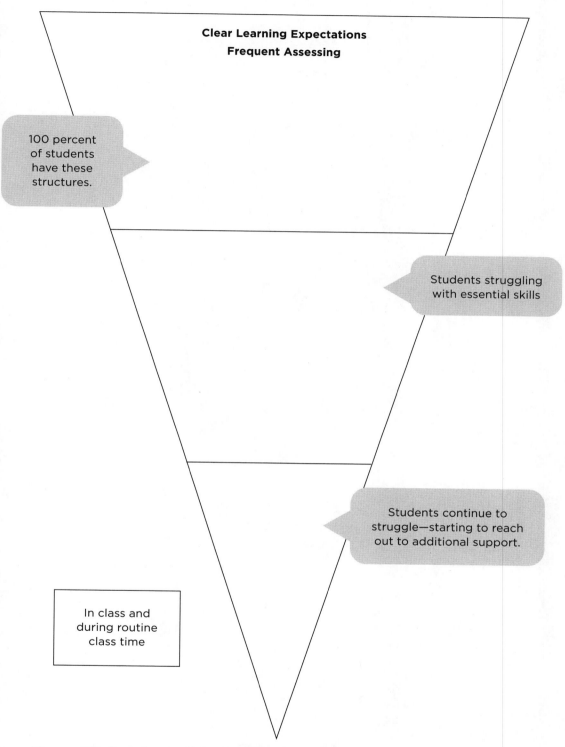

Figure 7.7: Developing classroom interventions.

*Visit **go.SolutionTree.com/PLCbooks** for a free reproducible version of this figure.*

EPILOGUE

Turning Parking Spaces Into Rest Spaces

In the video *Passion and Persistence*, Rick DuFour (2018) suggests it will take "passion and persistence" to become a PLC. DuFour says we should "recognize that the road to becoming a professional learning community is dotted with many tempting parking spaces." However, we must only rest in these spaces and then "push on!" because "obstacles and others can only stop you temporarily; you are the only one who can do it permanently." The wisdom in these statements is self-evident.

There are times when your CTE team might experience a hard learning curve while trying to establish interdependence—you might feel that the team should go back to old routines. Becoming a collaborative CTE team is a professional lifestyle change that takes time and effort. Until CTE teams fully embrace this new way of working together, such that collaboration is not just another thing added to an already busy day, there may be several bouts of resistance. However, reminding yourselves that career and technical education programs of study provide extremely important knowledge and skills should stave off the urge to park in one of those convenient spaces. Your school and district rely on your CTE team to prepare students to be job-ready graduates who are positive contributors to the larger community. Working within collaborative teams, even when not all members of the team teach the same content, provides a network, a support system, and a new pool of expertise that will strengthen the professional practice of each teacher on your team.

The steps your team must take toward becoming an interdependent collaborative team are not complex. However, becoming a team is not a thing to check off your list at the end of the school year. Becoming a team that makes a lasting impact on students learning the important life-long skills of career and technical education is a culture to cultivate. Growing this culture will take time, vulnerability, and a commitment to the collective professional growth of your team. It will take an enduring commitment to provide the best possible learning experience for all students your team serves.

APPENDIX A

Glossary of Terms

All students: Every student that your CTE team represents and is expected to be a self-sufficient member of society

Blended team: "A group of diverse professionals with a common purpose, appreciation, and understanding, who work collaboratively towards common student learning goals" (Custable, 2013, pp. 7–8)

Career and technical education (CTE): Formerly known as *vocational education*, these specialized courses prepare students with the applied, technical, and employability skills needed to be successful in college and career.

Collective inquiry: "The process of building shared knowledge by clarifying the questions that a group will explore together" (Cuddemi, 2019)

Common assessment: An assessment with the same questions and format, administered in the same window of time by two or more teachers

Common Core State Standards: A set of standards for the academic areas of mathematics and English language arts and literacy. Visit www.corestandards.org/about-the-standards to learn more.

CTE programs of study: Career and technical education courses offered in sixteen career clusters in the areas of agricultural education, business, marketing and computer education, family and consumer sciences, health sciences technology, and technology and engineering education

Employability skills: Transferable skills students learn in career and technical education courses that enable them to be successfully employable upon graduation from high school. Skills that will increase the likelihood of student employment, these skills are universal and applicable to most any type of employment and should be included in the delivery of CTE curricula. Employability skills include personal qualities, interpersonal skills, applied academic skills, critical thinking skills, resource management, information use, communication skills, systems thinking, and technology use.

Endurance skills: A skill that will prove to be valuable beyond a single test date. The student will learn the skill and apply the learning in the following months or beyond.

Essential learnings: Learner outcomes the team has vetted for essential eligibility, essential learnings must be learned by all students in the programs of study.

Essential skills: Skills, competencies, and learning outcomes that meet the endurance, leverage, and readiness criteria

Extension: In relation to student learning, it is an extension of the program of study's curriculum.

Formative assessment: An assessment that is used to inform instruction and student learning plans. This assessment takes place as part of (during) instruction, and the results provide guidance for the team, teacher, and students.

Four critical questions of a PLC:
1. What is it we want our students to know and be able to do?
2. How will we know each student has learned it?
3. How will we respond when some students do not learn it?
4. How will we extend the learning for students who have demonstrated proficiency?

Guaranteed and viable curriculum: The part of the curriculum that will be guaranteed for all students to have access to and learn. Primarily a combination of factors of an opportunity to learn and enough time for the students to learn it (Marzano, 2003).

High-stakes assessment: An assessment that is often administered at the end of the year or program of study; some are for state monitoring of student success and growth, and others are for certification purposes. The assessment is standardized so all students take the same assessment, with the same format, questions, and complexity.

High-stakes skills: A skill a student will learn that is connected to a high-stakes assessment and will prove to be valuable when the student takes a high-stakes assessment or to earn a certification

Intervention: "An intervention is anything a school does above and beyond what all students receive to help certain students succeed academically" (Buffum et al., 2018, p. 27).

Learning targets: An outcome from unwrapping a skill that clarifies in what way a student will learn a skill and provides guidance for assessing a student's learning

Leverage skill: A skill or learning outcome that will prove to be valuable in other disciplines. A skill the student learns in one class that gives him or her leverage, support, or an advantage in another class or in life.

Prevention: This takes place in Tier 1, in the classroom, by the classroom teacher or team of teachers. Prevention is provided to support student success and when successful, prevents the student from needing Tier 2 or 3 RTI support systems.

Professional learning community (PLC): Is "an ongoing process in which educators work collaboratively in recurring cycles of collective inquiry and action research to achieve better results for the students they serve" (DuFour, DuFour, Eaker, & Many, 2010, p. 11). PLC is *not* a team or a meeting!

Readiness skill: A skill or learner outcome that proves to be valuable for success in the next level of instruction, grade, college, postsecondary technical training for entering a career, or life.

Remediation: Support provided during the instructional day focused on below-grade-level curricula, foundational skills, and academic and social behaviors, in addition to receiving access to on-grade-level essential skills

Response to intervention (RTI): An inverted pyramid of support systems that are "built on the Professional Learning Community at Work® (PLC at Work®) process" (Buffum et al., 2018, p. v). RTI at Work™ is built on research-proven best practices to support struggling and high-achieving students.

Singletons: Programs of study or courses only taught by one teacher

Standard: Part of the curriculum that can include several skills, often written at the state or national level for programs of study in CTE

Success criteria: The course-specific knowledge and skills students need to master to be proficient with a learning target

Summative assessment: An assessment often administered at the end of a unit of instruction, semester, or year, also often used to give the student a final score or grade. Some may call a summative assessment in CTE an end-of-course (EOC) test.

Test blueprint: A document explaining the design and technical details of an assessment. Blueprints for high-stakes assessments are available in many states, but CTE teams can also create test blueprints for their own assessments.

Test technical guide: Similar to the test blueprint but may provide additional details about a publisher-created high-stakes or certification assessment

The right work: The right work of a CTE team is focused on the four critical questions of a PLC. CTE collaborative teams that always focus on increasing student learning are doing the right work.

Three big ideas of a PLC:
1. A focus on learning
2. A collaborative culture
3. A focus on results

Tight and loose: *Tight* refers to non-negotiables, things a team must do. *Loose* refers to things that are optional or for which there is some level of choice involved. For example, a team may agree to be tight regarding an essential skill all CTE students must learn and loose by agreeing teachers can teach the skill in a way that best fits their students. There should be an emphasis on the word *and*. Many people want things to be tight or loose. "A culture that is simultaneously loose and tight is one that empowers people to make important decisions and encourages them to be creative and innovative (loose), while at the same time, demands that certain aspects of the culture are nondiscretionary and required (tight)" (Mattos et al., 2016, p. 7).

Unpacking: A term that is synonymous with *deconstructing* and *unwrapping*. It means to "engage in a process that assists in developing instruction plans and assessments that leads to a better, more focused instruction and, ultimately, higher levels of learning for more students" (Friziellie, Schmidt, & Spiller, 2016, p. 46).

APPENDIX B

Reproducibles

Your team can use the reproducibles in this appendix to apply the concepts presented throughout the book.

- "Developing a Shared Vocabulary—The Three Big Ideas" (page 150)
- "Team Strengths and Growth Survey" (page 151)
- "Essential Learning Record Keeping" (page 153)
- "Unwrapping Essential Learnings" (page 154)
- "Scaled Learning Target" (page 155)
- "Instruction and Assessment Planning Guide" (page 156)
- "Guiding Questions for Establishing CTE Team SMART Goals" (page 157)
- "SMART Goal Appraisal" (page 158)
- "Question Strengths and Needs Protocol" (page 159)
- "Protocol for Auditing Assessment Items" (page 160)
- "Analyzing Questions Needing More Study Time" (page 161)
- "Protocol for Identifying Student Support Plans" (page 162)
- "Protocol for Informing Instructional Best Practices" (page 163)

Developing a Shared Vocabulary—
The Three Big Ideas

Record your individual definitions and team definitions from chapter 1 in the table below. Then capture the date of completion and list the names of all contributing team members.

This is an artifact of your team's efforts to collaboratively develop a shared vocabulary. This vocabulary should be referred to frequently until all members demonstrate a working knowledge and application of the vocabulary.

Each time a new member joins the team, the vocabulary should be reviewed and re-confirmed by the team, dated, and membership captured.

The Three Big Ideas		
Vocabulary of a PLC	**What are your independent definitions before reading about the terms?**	**What is your team's definition of each term?**
A Focus on Learning		
A Collaborative Culture and Collective Responsibility		
A Focus on Results		

Date of completion: _____

List the names of all contributing team members:

Collaboration for Career and Technical Education © 2020 Solution Tree Press • SolutionTree.com
Visit **go.SolutionTree.com/PLCbooks** to download this free reproducible.

Team Strengths and Growth Survey

Use the following six-step process to reach consensus on your team's strengths and areas for growth.

1. Independently rate each of the following twenty-two items.

2. Once all members of the team have completed their ratings, set a team meeting time to discuss the variations.

3. Develop a way for all members to share their ratings and rationale for their ratings on each item. Encourage them not to change their responses on an item until all members' scores on that item have been discussed.

4. After everyone on the team has been heard, collaboratively reach an agreement for each item's rating.

5. Celebrate the team's strengths.

6. Use results to identify a team action plan for growth.

The rating scale is 1—5: 1—Not true 2—Somewhat true 3—Pretty good—average 4—Above average 5—Great! Could be a model for others to see	Your Score	Team Score
Collaboration		
1. Our team collaboratively developed a statement of purpose for the team's existence and collaboration time.		
2. Our team develops and lives by our team norms and protocols to guide our collaboration time.		
3. Our team formally evaluates our adherence to team norms and the effectiveness of our team at least twice each year.		
4. Our team identifies SMART goals that require interdependency to achieve.		
5. Our team analyzes student achievement results to build our strengths and address our weaknesses to continuously improve our professional practice.		
Curriculum		
1. Each member on our team identifies the essential learnings lesson by lesson and unit by unit.		

page 1 of 2

Collaboration for Career and Technical Education © 2020 Solution Tree Press • SolutionTree.com
Visit **go.SolutionTree.com/PLCbooks** to download this free reproducible.

2. The essential learning outcomes identified by our team align with high-stakes assessments and certification requirements of our students.		
3. Our members have identified essential learning outcomes that overlap with one another.		
4. Our team has agreed how to best sequence the content for students to achieve the intended essential learnings.		
5. Our team identifies content and topics we can eliminate to devote more time to the essential curriculum.		
Assessment		
1. Our team creates assessments for prerequisite skills.		
2. Our team agrees on assessment format types.		
3. Our team agrees on assessment protocols before teaching the common essential learnings to be assessed.		
4. Our team agrees how they will judge student learning and assessment results before teaching the essential skills.		
5. Our team agrees on the frequency to administer team-developed assessments.		
6. Our team creates blueprints for our common assessments.		
7. Our team teaches students the criteria we use in judging the quality of their work and provides them with quality examples.		
Intervention		
1. Our team has developed strategies and systems to assist students lacking prerequisite knowledge and skills.		
2. Our assessment results are used to identify students needing additional support and extension.		
3. Our team shares and commits to in-class intervention systems.		
4. To benefit students, our team shares students to focus on essential learnings.		
5. Our team sets up intentional tutorial sessions and centers to help struggling students.		

*Source: Adapted from DuFour, R., DuFour, R., Eaker, R., Many, T. W., & Mattos, M. (2016).
Learning by doing: A handbook for Professional Learning Communities at Work (3rd ed.).
Bloomington, IN: Solution Tree Press.*

page 2 of 2

Essential Learning Record Keeping

Programs of Study	Essential Learning	Essential Criteria				Time Frame
		E	L	R	H	

E = Endurance   L = Leverage   R = Readiness   H = High Stakes

Unwrapping Essential Learnings

Program of Study:

Essential Learning Verbatim from the Curriculum Guide:

Essential Criteria—Does this standard meet at least three out of four criteria to be essential? Circle Yes or No.

Endurance	Leverage	Readiness	High Stakes
Yes or No	Yes or No	Yes or No	Yes or No

Endurance: Will this skill prove to be valuable beyond a single test date?

Leverage: Will this skill prove to be valuable in other disciplines?

Readiness: Will this skill prove to be valuable for success in the next level of instruction, grade, college, or entering a career?

High Stakes: Will this skill prove to be valuable when a student takes a high-stakes test or earns a certification?

Unwrap Essential Learnings

The process:

Highlight—Verbs

Underline—Knowledge-level components

Circle—Reasoning expectations explicit or implied

Box—Performance requirements

Star—Product development requirements

Highest level required learning target is: _____

Standard:

Skills Within the Standard	Learning Type			
	Knowledge	Reasoning	Performance	Product

Collaboration for Career and Technical Education © 2020 Solution Tree Press • SolutionTree.com

Visit **go.SolutionTree.com/PLCbooks** to download this free reproducible.

Scaled Learning Target

Programs:

Skill:

Learning Target:

4 Exceeding Mastery	3 Mastery	2 Approaching Mastery	1 Still Developing Mastery

Success Criteria:

Reflection on Learning:

Teacher Feedback:

Instruction and Assessment Planning Guide

Course Names:

Teachers Involved:	Start Date:	End Date:

ESSENTIAL SKILL:				
LEARNING TYPE:	Knowledge	Reasoning	Performance	Product
LEARNING TARGET:				

INSTRUCTION AND ASSESSMENT PLAN
What are the common assessment questions we want to ask to check students' learning of this essential skill?
What are the common lessons we will teach?

How will we respond when some students do not learn it?	How will we extend the learning for students who have demonstrated proficiency?

What is our instructional timeline for teaching this essential skill?

What might we do differently next time to improve this lesson?

Guiding Questions for Establishing CTE Team SMART Goals

SMART Goal Planning	
Where do we want to be?	
Where are we now?	
How will we get there?	
SMART Goal Reflecting	
What are we learning?	
Where should we focus next?	

SMART Goal Appraisal

Goal	S	M	A	R	T
	Strategic: Specific:				
	Strategic: Specific:				
	Strategic: Specific:				

Question Strengths and Needs Protocol

Teacher Name: _____ Content or Course: _____

Date Administered: _____

Question	Average Scores			Skill
	High	**Medium**	**Low**	
1.				
2.				
3.				
4.				
5.				

Protocol for Auditing Assessment Items

Teacher or Team Name: _____

Content or Course: _____

Date Administered: _____

Concerns About Questions					Questions to review, revise, or delete
	Other concerns	Depth of complexity	Format of the distractors	Format of the question stem	
					Question #
					Question #
					Question #

Analyzing Questions Needing More Study Time

Teacher or Team Name: _____

Content or Course: _____

Date Administered: _____

Issues and Questions to Review With Students					
Question numbers below 80 percent correct	Vocabulary of the question	Format of the question	Evidence of covering this	Other details to address	

Source: Adapted from Bailey, K., & Jakicic, C. (2012). Common formative assessment: A toolkit for Professional Learning Communities at Work. Bloomington, IN: Solution Tree Press.

Protocol for Identifying Student Support Plans

Teacher Name: _____

Content or Course: _____

Date Administered: _____

Question	Skill	Support Needed Students who score at developing mastery	Practice Needed Students who score at approaching mastery	More Challenge Needed Students who score at mastery or exceeding mastery

Source: Adapted from Bailey, K., & Jakicic, C. (2012). Common formative assessment: A toolkit for Professional Learning Communities at Work. Bloomington, IN: Solution Tree Press.

Collaboration for Career and Technical Education © 2020 Solution Tree Press • SolutionTree.com
Visit **go.SolutionTree.com/PLCbooks** to download this free reproducible.

Protocol for Informing Instructional Best Practices

The Discussion About Instructional Strategies That Had the Greatest Impact				
Teacher	**Highest performing test questions**	**Middle performing test questions**	**Low performing test questions**	

Source: Adapted from Bailey, K., & Jakicic, C. (2012). Common formative assessment: A toolkit for Professional Learning Communities at Work. Bloomington, IN: Solution Tree Press, pp. 112–113.

REFERENCES AND RESOURCES

ACT. (2017). *ACT Aspire technical manual* (Version 4). Iowa City, IA: Author. Accessed at http://ocs.archchicago.org/Portals/23/ACT%20Aspire%20Technical%20Manual%202017.pdf on February 25, 2020.

Adlai E. Stevenson High School. (2020). *Course syllabus—Marketing: BUS281 & BUS282.* Accessed at https://docs.google.com/document/d/1hL9-gkQCOW4KR9p90oG_B1eAn3M8hMOueNbBphEgbFk/edit on April 16, 2020.

Ainsworth, L. (2003). *Power standards: Identifying the standards that matter the most.* Denver, CO: Advanced Learning Press.

Ainsworth, L., & Viegut, D. (2006). *Common formative assessments: How to connect standards-based instruction and assessment.* Thousand Oaks, CA: Corwin Press.

Association for Career and Technical Education. (n.d.). *International CTE.* Accessed at www.acteonline.org/international-cte/ on February 7, 2020.

Bailey, K., & Jakicic, C. (2012). *Common formative assessment: A toolkit for Professional Learning Communities at Work.* Bloomington, IN: Solution Tree Press.

Bailey, K., & Jakicic, C. (2017). *Simplifying common assessment: A guide for Professional Learning Communities at Work.* Bloomington, IN: Solution Tree Press.

Black, P., & Wiliam, D. (1998). Inside the black box: Raising standards through classroom assessment. *Phi Delta Kappan, 92*(1). Accessed at www.academia.edu/2141639/Inside_the_black_box_Raising_standards_through_classroom_assessment on April 15, 2020.

Buffum, A., Mattos, M., & Malone, J. (2018). *Taking action: A handbook for RTI at Work.* Bloomington, IN: Solution Tree Press.

Buffum, A., Mattos M., & Weber, C. (2012). *Simplifying response to intervention: Four essential guiding principles.* Bloomington, IN: Solution Tree Press.

Burke, K. (2010). *Balanced assessment: From formative to summative.* Bloomington, IN: Solution Tree Press.

Carl D. Perkins Career and Technical Education Act of 2006. (2019, July 1). Accessed at https:// cte.careertech.org/sites/default/files/PerkinsV_September2018.pdf on November 7, 2019.

Carnevale, A., Jayasundera, T., & Hanson, A. (2012). *Career and technical education: Five ways that pay.* Washington, DC: Georgetown Public Policy Institute.

Collins, J., & Porras, J. (1997). *Built to last: Successful habits of visionary companies.* New York: Harper Business.

Common Core State Standards Initiative. (n.d.). *About the standards.* Accessed at www .corestandards.org/about-the-standards on November 7, 2019.

Conzemius, A., & O'Neill, J. (2014). *The handbook for SMART school teams: Revitalizing best practices for collaboration* (2nd ed.). Bloomington, IN: Solution Tree Press.

Cuddemi, J. (2019, February 20). Maybe it's time to press the reset button. *AllThingsPLC.* Accessed at www.allthingsplc.info/blog/view/377/maybe-its-time-to-press-the-reset -button on February 25, 2020.

Custable, W. (2013). *How do professional learning communities foster strong career and technical education programs of study in Illinois public high schools?* Unpublished doctoral dissertation, Loyola University, Chicago. Accessed at http://ecommons.luc.edu/cgi /viewcontent.cgi?article=1510&context=luc_diss on November 5, 2019.

Custable, W. (2019). Implementing proficiency-based grading in career and technical education. In A. R. Reibel & E. Twadell (Eds.), *Proficiency-based grading in the content areas: Insights and key questions for secondary schools* (pp. 35–57). Bloomington, IN: Solution Tree Press.

DuFour, R. (2003). Leading edge: 'Collaboration lite' puts student achievement on a starvation diet. *Journal of Staff Development, 24*(3), 63–64.

DuFour, R. (2018). *Passion and persistence* [Video]. Bloomington, IN: Solution Tree Press.

DuFour, R., & DuFour, R. (2012). *The school leader's guide to Professional Learning Communities at Work.* Bloomington, IN: Solution Tree Press.

DuFour, R., DuFour, R., & Eaker, R. (2008). *Revisiting Professional Learning Communities at Work: New insights for improving schools.* Bloomington, IN: Solution Tree Press.

DuFour, R., DuFour, R., Eaker, R., & Many, T. (2010). *Learning by doing: A handbook for Professional Learning Communities at Work* (2nd ed.). Bloomington, IN: Solution Tree Press.

DuFour, R., DuFour, R., Eaker, R., Many, T. W., & Mattos, M. (2016). *Learning by doing: A handbook for Professional Learning Communities at Work* (3rd ed.). Bloomington, IN: Solution Tree Press.

DuFour, R., Eaker, R., & DuFour, R. (Eds.). (2005). *On common ground: The power of professional learning communities.* Bloomington, IN: Solution Tree Press.

DuFour, R., & Marzano, R. J. (2011). *Leaders of learning: How district, school, and classroom leaders improve student achievement.* Bloomington, IN: Solution Tree Press.

Erkens, C., Jakicic, C., Jessie, L., King, D., Kramer, S. V., Many, T., et al. (2008). *The collaborative teacher: Working together as a professional learning community.* Bloomington, IN: Solution Tree Press.

Erkens, C., & Twadell, E. (2012). *Leading by design: An action framework for PLC at Work leaders.* Bloomington, IN: Solution Tree Press.

Friziellie, H., Schmidt, J., & Spiller, J. (2016). *Yes we can! General and special educators collaborating in a professional learning community.* Bloomington, IN: Solution Tree Press.

Gabriel, J., & Farmer, P. (2009). *How to help your school thrive without breaking the bank.* Alexandria, VA: Association for Supervision and Curriculum Development.

Georgia Department of Education. (2019). Career, technical and agricultural Education. Accessed at www.gadoe.org/Curriculum-Instruction-and-Assessment/CTAE/Pages/default.aspx on February 20, 2020.

The Glossary of Education Reform. (2014, April 29). *Career and technical education.* Accessed at www.edglossary.org/career-and-technical-education/ on January 26, 2020.

Goodwin, B., & Hubbell, E. R. (2013). *The 12 touchstones of good teaching: A checklist for staying focused every day.* Alexandria, VA: Association for Supervision and Curriculum Development.

Goodwin, B., & Miller, K. (2013). Research says / Nonfiction reading promotes student success. *Educational Leadership, 70*(4), 80–82. Accessed at www.ascd.org/publications/educational-leadership/dec12/vol70/num04/Nonfiction-Reading-Promotes-Student-Success.aspx on February 25, 2020.

Gregory, G., Kaufeldt, M., & Mattos, M. (2016). *Best practices at tier 1: Daily differentiation for effective instruction, secondary.* Bloomington, IN: Solution Tree Press.

Hansen, A. (2015). *How to develop PLCs for singletons and small schools.* Bloomington, IN: Solution Tree Press.

Hattie, J. (2009). *Visible learning: A synthesis of over 800 meta-analyses related to achievement.* New York: Routledge.

Lencioni, P. (2002). *The five dysfunctions of a team: A leadership fable.* San Francisco: Jossey-Bass.

Marzano, R. J. (2003). *What works in schools: Translating research into action.* Alexandria, VA: Association for Supervision and Curriculum Development.

Marzano, R. J. (2017). *The new art and science of teaching.* Bloomington, IN: Solution Tree Press.

Marzano, R. J., Norford, J. S., & Ruyle, M. (2019). *The new art and science of classroom assessment.* Bloomington, IN: Solution Tree Press.

Marzano, R. J., Warrick P., & Simms, J. A. (2014). *A handbook for high reliability schools: The next step in school reform.* Bloomington, IN: Solution Tree Press.

Mattos, M., DuFour, R., DuFour, R., & Eaker, R. (2016). *Concise answers to frequently asked questions about Professional Larning Communities at Work*. Bloomington, IN: Solution Tree Press.

Moss, C., & Brookhart, S. (2012). *Learning targets: Helping students aim for understanding in today's lesson*. Alexandria, VA: Association for Supervision and Curriculum Development.

Muhammad, A. (2009). *Transforming school culture: How to overcome staff division*. Bloomington, IN: Solution Tree Press.

National Association of State Administrators of Family and Consumer Sciences. (2018). *Family & consumer sciences national standards 3.0*. Accessed at www.nasafacs.org/uploads /1/8/3/9/18396981/fcs_national_standards_3.0_complete_6-12-17.pdf on February 25, 2020.

Office of the State Superintendent of Education. (n.d.). *The Common Career Technical Core (CCTC)*. Accessed at https://osse.dc.gov/service/common-career-technical-core-cctc on November 8, 2019.

Organisation for Economic Co-operation and Development. (2014). *Education at a glance 2014*. Accessed at www.oecd.org/edu/United%20States-EAG2014-Country-Note.pdf on November 8, 2019.

Patterson, P., Grenny, J., Maxfield, D., McMillan, R., & Switzler, A. (2008). *Influencer: The power to change anything*. New York: McGraw-Hill.

Perkins Collaborative Resource Network. (n.d.a). *Employability skills*. Accessed at https://cte .ed.gov/initiatives/employability-skills-framework on November 8, 2019.

Perkins Collaborative Resource Network. (n.d.b). *Perkins v*. Accessed at https://cte.ed.gov /legislation/perkins-v on November 8, 2019.

Reeves, D. B. (2002). *The leader's guide to standards: A blueprint for educational equity and excellence*. San Francisco: Jossey-Bass.

Reeves, D. B. (2003). *High performance in high poverty schools: 90/90/90 and beyond*. Englewood, CO: Center for Performance Assessment.

Reeves, D. B. (2004). *Accountability for learning: How teachers and school leaders can take charge*. Alexandria, VA: Association for Supervision and Curriculum Development.

Reibel, A., & Twadell, E. (2019). *Proficiency-based grading in the content areas: Insights and key questions for secondary schools*. Bloomington, IN: Solution Tree Press.

Stevenson High School. (n.d.). Vision and values / Portrait of a graduate. Accessed at www .d125.org/about/vision-and-values-portrait-of-a-graduate on February 25, 2020.

Stump, S. (2019, February 1). *Envisioning 21st century career and technical education* [Video file]. Washington, DC: Department of Education. Accessed at https://cte.ed.gov /legislation/perkins-v on February 25, 2020.

U.S. Department of Education. (2019, September). *Bridging the skills gap: Career and technical education in high school.* Accessed at www2.ed.gov/datastory/cte/index .html#data-story-title on February 3, 2020.

Virginia Department of Education CTE Resource Center. (2019a). *Accounting task /competency list.* Accessed at www.cteresource.org/verso/courses/6320/accounting-tasklist on February 3, 2020.

Virginia Department of Education CTE Resource Center. (2019b). *Agriscience and technology task/competency list.* Accessed at www.cteresource.org/verso/courses/8001/agriscience -technology-tasklist on February 3, 2020.

Virginia Department of Education CTE Resource Center. (2019c). *Business management task/competency list.* Accessed at www.cteresource.org/verso/courses/6136/business -management-tasklist on February 25, 2020.

Virginia Department of Education CTE Resource Center. (2019d). *Construction technology computer/technology standards of learning.* Accessed at www.cteresource.org/verso/course s/8432/construction-technology-ctsols on February 25, 2020.

Virginia Department of Education CTE Resource Center. (2019e). *Family and consumer sciences exploratory I task/competency list.* Accessed at www.cteresource.org/verso/courses/8207 /family-and-consumer-sciences-exploratory-i-tasklist on February 3, 2020.

Virginia Department of Education CTE Resource Center. (2019f). *Home health aide task /competency list.* Accessed at www.cteresource.org/verso/courses/8364/home-health-aide -tasklist on February 3, 2020.

Virginia Department of Education CTE Resource Center. (2019g). *Industrial maintenance technology I task/competency list.* Accessed at www.cteresource.org/verso/courses/8575 /industrial-maintenance-technology-i-tasklist on February 25, 2020.

Virginia Department of Education CTE Resource Center. (2019h). *Plumbing I task /competency list.* Accessed at www.cteresource.org/verso/courses/8551/plumbing-i-tasklist on February 25, 2020.

Virginia Department of Education CTE Resource Center. (2019i). *Small animal care I task /competency list.* Accessed at www.cteresource.org/verso/courses/8083/small-animal-care-i -tasklist on February 3, 2020.

Virginia Department of Education CTE Resource Center. (2019j). *Virginia's CTE resource center—Career and technical education.* Accessed at www.cteresource.org on February 3, 2020.

Williams, K., & Hierck, T. (2015). *Starting a movement: Building culture from the inside out in professional learning communities.* Bloomington, IN: Solution Tree Press.

INDEX

Learning by Doing, Third Edition
Richard DuFour, Rebecca DuFour, Robert Eaker,
Thomas W. Many, and Mike Mattos
Discover how to transform your school or district into a
high-performing PLC. The third edition of this comprehensive
action guide offers new strategies for addressing critical PLC
topics, including hiring and retaining new staff, creating
team-developed common formative assessments, and more.
BKF746

How to Develop PLCs for Singletons and Small Schools
Aaron Hansen
Ensure singleton teachers feel integrally involved in the
PLC process. With this user-friendly guide, you'll discover
how small schools, full of singleton teachers who are the
only ones in their schools teaching their subject areas, can
build successful PLCs.
BKF676

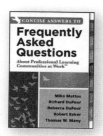

Concise Answers to Frequently Asked Questions About Professional Learning Communities at Work®
Mike Mattos, Richard DuFour, Rebecca DuFour,
Robert Eaker, and Thomas W. Many
Get all of your PLC questions answered. Designed as a
companion resource to *Learning by Doing: A Handbook for
Professional Learning Communities at Work®* (3rd ed.), this
powerful, quick-reference guidebook is a must-have for
teachers and administrators working to create and sustain
the PLC process.
BKF705

Help Your Team
Michael D. Bayewitz, Scott A. Cunningham, Joseph A. Ianora,
Brandon Jones, Maria Nielsen, Will Remmert, Bob Sonju,
and Jeanne Spiller
Written by eight PLC at Work® experts, this practical guide
addresses the most common challenges facing collaborative
teams. Each chapter offers a variety of templates, processes, and
strategies to help your team resolve conflict, focus on the right
work, and take collective responsibility for student success.
BKF886

Solution Tree | Press

a division of
Solution Tree

Visit SolutionTree.com or call 800.733.6786 to order.

"Tremendous, tremendous, tremendous!

The speaker made me do some very deep internal reflection about the **PLC process** and the personal responsibility I have in making the school improvement process work **for ALL kids.**"

— Marc Rodriguez, teacher effectiveness coach, Denver Public Schools, Colorado

PD Services

Our experts draw from decades of research and their own experiences to bring you practical strategies for building and sustaining a high-performing PLC. You can choose from a range of customizable services, from a one-day overview to a multiyear process.

Book your PLC PD today!
888.763.9045

Solution Tree